Narrating Their Lives: Examining English Language Teachers' Professional Identities within the Classroom

Lía D. Kamhi-Stein, Editor
California State University, Los Angeles

Foreword by Stephanie Vandrick

Ann Arbor
The University of Michigan Press

Published in the United States of America
The University of Michigan Press
Manufactured in the United States of America

♾ Printed on acid-free paper

ISBN-13: 978-0-472-03499-4

2016 2015 2014 2013 4 3 2 1

Library of Congress Cataloging-in-Publication Data

Kamhi-Stein, Lía D.

English language teachers narrating their lives : from the construction of professional identities to the construction of the language classroom / Lia D. Kamhi-Stein, PhD.

pages cm.

"Educational Sociolinguistics" presented at the 2007 Annual Conference of the California Teachers of English to Speakers of Other Languages (CATESOL)."

Includes bibliographical references and index.

ISBN 978-0-472-12014-7 (cloth : alk. paper) -- ISBN 978-0-472-03499-4 (pbk. : alk. paper)

1. English teachers--Training of--Social aspects 2. English teachers--Self-rating of. 3. English teachers--Training of--Research--Methodology. 4. Identity (Psychology)--Social aspects. 5. English language--Study and teaching--Foreign speakers--Evaluation. 6. Second language acquisition--Research--Methodology. 7. Communication in education—Social aspects. 8. Language and education. I. Title.

PE1066.K36 2013

428.0071—dc23

Narrating Their Lives: Examining English Language Teachers' Professional Identities within the Classroom

Dedication

A mi marido, Alan Paul Stein (1947–2008), que me enseñó que se puede vivir y morir con dignidad. I know he's smiling at me from up there.

Acknowledgments

Usually in this section, authors and editors thank people who helped them complete their book projects. In my case, I have a long list of people who actually helped me find renewed strength when I was going through a very difficult time in my life. This book project began in 2007. For the spring quarter of 2008, I received a California State University, Los Angeles (CSULA) Creative Leave Award that would give me the time needed to finish this book. However, as John Lennon well put it, "Life is what happens to you when you are busy making other plans." My plan was to complete this book that quarter, but what happened was that my husband's cancer took a turn for the worse and he died in May of 2008. At that time, I had a wonderful two-year old daughter (who is six years old now) to take care of, a full-time job that kept me as focused as I could be at that time, and the responsibility of a life on my own. And the book project, you might ask? Well, it took a while to complete it, but now it is done, and I believe that time gave me a much better perspective about the book's content.

Therefore, in this section, I must thank CSULA for the Creative Leave Award that enabled me to work on this book. Second, a huge thank you to Veneza Angel Pablico, Hee-Jin Kim, Jessie Chen, Jeremy C. Kelley, Valerie J. Callet, and Shannon Ladymon, the authors of the autobiographical narratives contained in this book. I want to thank them for their incredible patience and support as I worked in the project. Third, another huge thanks to Carol Ayers, a former student of mine who is a professional editor in the healthcare field. Carol volunteered to work with the authors as their autobiographical narratives went through several editorial stages. Carol was always ready to volunteer her time and energy and help me through difficult times. Fourth, thank you to Jonathan Loh, another former student who helped me frame some of the questions in two chapters in the book. Fifth, thank you to Flora Birdzell and Jennifer Kagawa for their work on the indexes. Sixth, I am grateful to the many pre-service teachers in my Educational Sociolinguistics class who shared their autobiographical narratives with me. Their strength, courage, and determination to achieve inspired me to work on this book. Seventh, I want to thank the anonymous reviewer commissioned by the University of Michigan Press whose positive comments and constructive feedback made me feel that I was onto something. Eighth and foremost, I want to thank Kelly Sippell. I am indebted to her for her patience, understanding, and huge support. I also want to thank her for her feedback through the many phases of this project. Thank you, Kelly!

On a personal note, I want to acknowledge my daughter, Hannah Malena Stein, whose strength and unconditional love are a source of daily inspiration and happiness. Finally, I want to thank my husband for many years of love and personal and professional support. He asked me to dedicate this book to him and now that the book is completed, I have fulfilled my promise. Thank you, Alan!

Foreword by Stephanie Vandrick

I am truly pleased to welcome this groundbreaking book, *Narrating Their Lives: Examining English Language Teachers' Professional Identities within the Classroom*. As someone who has herself written about educators' identities and about personal narratives as a genre of scholarship, I consider these two topics, and the ways they intersect, essential to our understanding in the field of TESOL, and especially important to raise in TESOL teacher education programs. This book deserves to be read widely, taught, and discussed by teacher educators and teachers everywhere, not only because of the importance of the interrelated and timely topics, but also because its narratives reach out to readers, drawing us in and helping us understand teachers of the various and linguistic and racial identities in today's schools. This is one of those rare professional books that light up both our minds and our hearts.

The first issue that author Lía Kamhi-Stein focuses on is that an important element in education today is teacher identities, especially linguistic identities. She understands that today's teachers, including English language teachers, often have more diverse and less easily classified ethnic, racial, linguistic, and other identities than was true in the past; she also understands that this diversity is a great resource for our schools. The second issue she focuses on is that one of the best ways to convey this diversity of teacher identities is through autobiographical narrative, a genre that is becoming increasingly common in academe, although still not widely found in TESOL publications. There is a power, an immediacy, in these narratives that speaks directly to readers.

A unique and central feature of this book is its six narratives by classroom teachers (as well as a brief autobiographical narrative by Kamhi-Stein herself to set the stage for the teachers' narratives). As the author points out, most of the few personal narratives in TESOL (and elsewhere) so far have been by and about university scholars and researchers rather than K–12 classroom teachers. I would add that other personal narratives that have been published are narratives of students, narratives *about* the classroom, and narratives by researchers about classroom teachers (thus in a sense taking the shaping of the narratives into their hands rather than allowing the teachers to tell their own stories as they do in this book). Education scholars such as Clandinin (e.g., 1992) and Florio-Ruane (2001), and TESOL teacher education scholars such as Johnson and Golombek (2002) have written about personal narrative. Personal narratives are also sometimes addressed in teacher education discussions of teacher cognition (e.g., Borg, 2003) or teacher reflection or reflexivity (e.g., Edge, 2010). Finally, such autobiographical narratives are sometimes employed in unpublished teacher education class materials and assignments. All of these provide context for, and lay the groundwork for, this book, in which the six teachers write their own narratives about their own identities and how these identities intersect with and influence their teaching lives.

Autobiographical narratives should not simply tell stories; narratives need to be thoughtful and analytical and need to address issues that are important to the discipline; those in this book fulfill these requirements. These autobiographical stories shed light not just on the lives of specific individuals, but on certain themes that are relevant in a much broader way. The stories provide concrete, engaging illustrations of concepts and terms often taught in teacher preparation classes. One central theme or issue is that of the roles of native English speaker (NES) instructors and nonnative English speaker teachers (NNESTs). Unfortunately, there are still some employers and others who favor, or even limit themselves to, NES instructors, believing that they will be better teachers and that students will prefer them. Fortunately, this attitude is changing somewhat, as a result of advocacy and research showing that well-prepared NNESTs not only share professional competence with well-prepared NES instructors, but also have some distinct advantages, such as understanding the students' second language learning process better. Three of the contributors to this book, NNESTs themselves, write candidly about their experiences with these issues in the first grouping of narratives, "autobiographies of transnational teachers from the expanding circle."

These three contributors' narratives also illustrate a related issue: the difficulty of definitively categorizing individuals into native or nonnative speakers of English, or of any language, when in today's world, there are so many who have moved back and forth among countries, schools, and languages. For example, Veneza Angel Pablico was born in the Philippines, was surrounded with Tagalog speakers, spoke English and "Taglish" with her family, and then moved to the U.S.A.; she asks herself if she is a NES instructor or a NNEST and decides she is a "bilingual or a multicompetent speaker." Or consider Hee-Jin Kim, who was born in Korea, moved to the U.S.A. at the age of six, returned to Korea at age 12, studied German in college, and spent a year in Germany, and now describes herself as "a nonnative English–speaking Korean female with a U.S. accent who studied German." And Jessie Chen, who has lived in three different countries, feels she is "part of a transnational diaspora" and a "cultural hybrid," telling us that she is "Korean by birth, American by law, Chinese by association, and all of the above and beyond geopolitically and socioculturally." Not only teachers, but also their students, are often hard to categorize; this is a reality that must be recognized in educational settings, perhaps most crucially in teacher preparation programs, where attitudes and understandings set the tone for teachers' careers and classrooms. This book is a resource that will aid in that adaptation.

Adding depth to the book is the fact that the included stories and issues are not limited to those of the three NNESTs (or some variation thereof) in the first grouping. There are also narratives from three NES instructors, all of whom recount language and/or culture-related issues or teaching situations that they feel affect their teaching and how they are perceived; these are grouped in a section on "problematizing the notion of 'inner circle legitimacy'" (using Kachru's three-circle model of English use throughout the world). Jeremy C. Kelley found that when he moved to the North, his Southern accent was sometimes a liability; this caused him both to make changes in his own self-presentation and to ponder his role in his work experiences. The other two "inner circle" writers deal mostly with race; they are white teachers teaching predominantly non-white students, and they try to understand the tangled connections between race and native speaker status. Valerie J. Callet wonders how she can reconcile feeling "ashamed and guilty of my own race" with being an effective and caring teacher for all her students. Shannon Ladymon, whose parents divorced when she was an infant and who shared custody of her, went back and forth between Texas and California every few months, constantly adapting "my dialect, my body language, my actions…in order to seem like I fit in." It is a strength of this book that the stories included cover a range of identity issues to do with race, ethnicity, language, and culture, rather than strictly preserving the more commonly cited dichotomy between instructors who are native speakers and those who are nonnative speakers.

The structure of the book, highlighting but also providing context and scholarly support for the narratives, serves to reinforce its effectiveness and accessibility. There are still some who doubt the contributions that personal narrative can make to scholarship and to practice. I believe that this book provides powerful evidence that personal narrative can make strong, important, and very readable contributions to the field of TESOL and beyond. There is something compelling about narratives, or as Coles (1990) puts it, about "the call of stories." Teacher educators, teachers, and other readers respond strongly and positively to such narratives, making connections and enhancing their understanding of concepts. In teacher preparation classes, the narratives in this book can complement the more expository and/or theoretical publications that students are reading. I know of several teacher educators who seek out and use such narratives in order to introduce or elucidate important topics, and who will welcome publication of this volume. Kamhi-Stein's chapters on pedagogy, both for language and teacher preparation classes, enhance the usefulness of the narratives.

The carefully wrought blend of personal narrative and support from scholarly literature makes this book ideal for use in teacher education classrooms, and an important book for teachers and teacher educators. I am eager to see it go out into the world and engage, inform, and connect with present and future teachers and teacher educators.

References

Borg, S. (2003). Teacher cognition in language teaching: A review of research on what language teachers think, know, believe and do. *Language Teaching, 36*(2), 81–109.

Clandinin, D. J. (1992). Narrative and story in teacher education. In T. Russell & H. Munby (Eds.), *Teachers and teaching: From classroom to reflection* (pp. 121–134). New York: Routledge.

Coles, R. (1989). The call of stories: Teaching and the moral imagination. Boston: Houghton Mifflin.

Edge, J. (2010). *The reflexive teacher educator in TESOL: Roots and wings.* New York: Routledge.

Florio-Ruane, S. (2001). *Teacher education and the cultural imagination: Autobiography, conversation, and narrative.* New York: Routledge.

Johnson, K. E., & Golombek, P. R. (Eds.). (2002). *Teachers' narrative inquiry as professional development.* New York: Cambridge University Press.

Contents

Introduction

Do you see a relationship between your personal and professional identities and your actions (or non-actions) in the classroom? If so, can you describe the relationship?

◆ Why This Book?

"How can I use your experiences to help my second language learners succeed?"

This book was prompted by this question, asked by an ESL teacher who was attending a presentation given by an elementary school teacher—a former student of mine—at the 2007 California Teachers of English to Speakers of Other Languages (CATESOL) annual conference. The presenter, who had immigrated from El Salvador to the U.S. at the age of 17, showcased the autobiographical narrative she had written in TESL 570, Educational Sociolinguistics, a required class that I teach in the Master's Program in Teaching English to Speakers of Other Languages (MA in TESOL) at California State University, Los Angeles. Central to her autobiographical narrative was a discussion of how her professional and personal identities contributed to helping her to implement "a pedagogy of empowerment" (to use Amin's, 2004 term, p. 72)—that is, pedagogical practices that disrupt the notion that one needs to be white and a native speaker of English in order to teach the language.

Since the publication of Norton's (also known as Peirce) (see Norton, 1997; Peirce, 1995; Norton, 2000) seminal work focusing on language learner identity, the field of TESOL has paid increased attention to how issues of race and ethnicity, language status and cultural background, and issues of power affect the process of identity negotiation and construction among second language learners. More recently, interest in issues of identity has focused on teachers and pre-service teachers (see the work of Belcher & Connor, 2001; Curtis & Romney, 2006; Liu, 2004; Morita, 2004; Nunan & Choi, 2010; Pavlenko, 2003; Varghese et al., 2005). Though the work on language teacher identity is extremely informative, valuable, and thought provoking, with the exceptions of Liu (2004) and Morita (2004), it has not explicitly dealt with the relationship between personal and professional identity and language teaching.

Additionally, the volumes published on language teacher identity have primarily focused on highly accomplished academics (see Curtis & Romney, 2006; Nunan & Choi, 2010). Without a doubt, much can be learned from reading about the experiences of highly successful professionals in the field; however, the reality is that teachers of ELLs may not necessarily see their experiences reflected in those of academics and researchers. The purpose of this book, then, is to examine the process of identity construction of *classroom teachers,* who are in daily contact with language learners, in order to uncover the connections between teachers' personal and professional identities and their instructional practices[1]. The heuristic used to uncover the connections is the autobiographical narrative, a form of narrative inquiry that has recently become an established source of research in SLA.

In writing this book, my intention was to use language that would be accessible to a wide audience that includes professionals who are novices to the topic of language teacher identity or busy teachers who, though they may be interested in the topic, may not have the time to become immersed in it. While I find the published books and articles on the topic to be excellent, they are not necessarily accessible to read-

[1]I should note that, although at the time the authors wrote their narratives when they were teaching in the classroom, a couple of them went on to obtain higher education degrees and are currently working as K–12 administrators or initiating their careers in academia.

ers who are new to the topic. This book is also designed to be accessible to pre-service teachers who may be interested in learning about issues of language teacher identity as well as to pre-service teacher educators who may want to integrate the topic into their credential or teacher preparation courses.

This Introduction discusses the two topics that are central to this book—language teacher identity and narrative research.

◆ Exploring Language Teacher Identity: Seminal and Recent Research

> The frustration I felt throughout my school years in the United States contributed to my decision to become an educator in the field of TESOL. I felt that being in ESL classes that did not promote the development of academic language proficiency prevented me from acquiring academic skills that were necessary to pursue a career. Therefore, as an educator, I am committed to providing my students with academic instruction so that they will acquire not only BICS but, most importantly, CALP (Cummins, 1996). My ultimate goal as a teacher is to increase my students' opportunities to pursue higher education.

It is not common practice to open a section designed to summarize research with a quotation, in this case a quotation from an autobiographical narrative written by Patty Garcia, an immigrant from Mexico who currently works as a middle school teacher for the Los Angeles Unified School District. However, Patty's quotation is relevant because it encompasses, at least in part, what the research has to say about language teachers' identity: That teachers' lives and learning histories have a deep effect on their beliefs about teaching and learning and their positionality in the classroom. Two other aspects of teacher identity, which are not reflected in the quotation, are that (1) a person's identity is not fixed, stable, or one and the same throughout life but is instead multi-faceted, shifting, and often times contradictory (Peirce, 1995; Weedon, 1987) and (2) agency plays an important role in the process of identity construction (Morita, 2004; Losey, 1995; Varghese et al., 2005).

To my knowledge, two of the first articles that focused on language teacher identity were published in the special topic issue of *TESOL Quarterly* edited by Bonny Norton (1997), titled *Language and Identity*. The first article was an ethnographic study conducted by Duff and Uchida (1997), focusing on four EFL teachers in Japan. The results of the study showed that the teachers' sociocultural identities were affected by their: "(a) past learning experience, (b) past teaching experiences, and (c) cross-cultural experiences" (p. 468). However, the teachers' identities were also affected by the educational context in which they were embedded (a private EFL institute), the classes they taught, the instructional materials they used, and their students and colleagues. The second article (Amin, 1997, see also 2004 for a follow-up study on the same topic) was seminal since it was likely the first one to complexify the relationship between language teachers' race and language. Amin's (1997) study concluded that when language learners do not perceive their teachers to be legitimate because the teachers are visible minorities and may be second language speakers, the teachers' identities suffer and they are unable to present themselves as effective professionals. In turn, these negative self-perceptions result in instructional practices that are not as strong as they could be.

More recently, Motha (2006) conducted another study designed to complexify the relationship between race and language teacher identity. This time, the study investigated how four new native English-speaking female teachers—three white and one Korean-American—negotiated their racial identities in U.S. schools. Motha provided a rich description of how the teachers challenged their school cultures that silently privileged the notions of whiteness and standard American English. In a foreign language setting in China, Tsui's (2007) narrative inquiry resulted in a detailed description of the struggles that one nonnative English-speaking EFL teacher faced when he adopted communicative language teaching (CLT) because it was the sanctioned approach, even though he questioned the effectiveness of CLT because of his own EFL learning experience. Eventually, the teacher adapted CLT to meet his own as well as his students' beliefs and expectations.

The topic of language teacher identity has also been the focus of recent dissertation research. This line of work, which has mainly dealt with how nonnative English–speaking teachers (NNESTs) construct and negotiate their identities, can be attributed to the growing interest in NNESTs since Braine's seminal work (Braine et al., 1996; Braine, 1999) and the establishment of the NNEST caucus in TESOL (Braine, Liu, & Kamhi-Stein, 1998). Overall, these dissertations show that the process of constructing a professional identity is not linear or simple. They also show that the setting in which teachers function has an impact on how teachers perceive themselves (a point made by Samimy & Brutt-Griffler, 1999, and more recently by Chang, 2004; Choi, 2007; Lu, 2005; Saito, 2005).

More specifically, Saito's (2005) dissertation, which focused on five graduate students who were teaching composition at a U.S. university, shows that, in the process of identity construction, the teachers experienced adaptive cultural transformation—including the ability to "communicate appropriately and effectively in the target culture by expanding his or her social identity to one that blends the new set of values, habits, and social norms endorsed in the target culture with those in the home language" (Liu, 2004, p. 37). At the same time, the teachers showed resistance, which allowed them to use a "counter-discourse in order to reframe power relations between themselves and their students" (Saito, 2005, p. 292). The study also showed that as the teachers became more confident professionals, their identities did not remain static, but changed and developed. Lu's (2005) dissertation investigated the process of professional identity construction of four NNESTs of K–12 and identified five obstacles that people face in navigating their professional lives: visibility, resource, barrier, resistance, and sabotage (Stenberg & Spear-Swerling, 1998, cited in Lu, 2005).

In yet another study focusing on transnational developing NNESTs who were teaching academic writing to international students in a U.S. university, Choi (2007) found that the teachers' self-perceptions and positioning in the classroom were dependent on positive perceptions about their authority (in the case of a male teacher from Central Asia) or negative perceptions (in the case of the two female participants, one from Korea and the other one from China). The study also showed that self-perceptions of English competency affected their identity as professionals and that age and nationality affected the teachers differently (with the Korean teacher perceiving herself to be too young to teach Korean students who were older than her, and the Chinese teacher not perceiving age or nationality to be a problem). The male teacher from Central Asia believed that his nationality—and most probably his multicultural background—was a strength since he felt it contributed to his instructional practices. The study also showed that the teachers viewed the relationship between race and language similarly. Specifically, the three teachers believed that their students associated race with language status: for them looking (or not looking) Asian led their students to perceive them as native or nonnative speakers. This finding supports Amin's (1997) notion that visible minority teachers are often perceived as not being legitimate as teachers. One interesting point in Choi's study is that while the three teachers did not necessarily "buy into" the native speaker fallacy, the teachers' belief systems were still "subtly and silently" affected by it.

The one study in an EFL setting investigated teachers in Taiwan (Chang, 2004). Much like the other dissertations, this study concluded that how teachers constructed their professional identities was affected by their educational and personal experiences. Additionally, the study showed that the teachers, all NNESTs, did not believe that one needs to be a native speaker of English to be a good teacher. This confirms findings by Samimy and Brutt-Griffler (1999), who found that the professionals they investigated—graduate students who were mostly very experienced EFL teachers before coming to the U.S.—had not perceived their status as a NNEST to be a problem.

Work on language teacher identity has also focused on language teacher education programs. Specifically, five studies (Samimy & Brutt-Griffler, 1999; Chacón, 2009; Golombek & Jordan, 2005; Ilieva,

2010; Pavlenko, 2003) have investigated the role that critical praxis can play in helping graduate students deconstruct colonial notions of native speakerness and whiteness. Taken together, the studies show that language teacher preparation programs can play a critical role in helping graduate students see themselves as belonging to communities of L2 users (rather than L2 learners or nonnative speakers). Of particular interest is the study by Pavlenko (2003), which introduced Wenger's notion of "imagined communities" involving "any community of practice an individual may want to seek entrance into" (Pavlenko, 2003, p. 253). Pavlenko concluded that the readings students completed on the topics of bilingualism and multicompetence (rather than on issues that are part of the native–nonnative speaker dichotomy) allowed language minority teachers to see themselves as belonging to imagined communities describing them as legitimate L2 users (rather than L2 learners). Another relevant study investigated how international students asserted their identities as legitimate teachers of English in a pronunciation course titled "Teaching American English Pronunciation." The results of the study by Golombek and Jordan (2005) were similar to those by Pavlenko (2003) in that while the two participating students were influenced by the notion of the native speaker being white, the readings to which they were exposed that challenged the myth of the native speaker, gave them an opportunity to take on an identity of legitimate teachers and users of English. A third noteworthy study is the one by Chacón (2009), conducted in an Expanding Circle context, which showed that a course designed to bring student awareness about racialization promoted thinking about the students' attitudes toward and biases about issues of race.

In summary, research on language teacher identity supports the notion that teachers' perceptions (those of self and others), their beliefs about teaching and language status, and factors like the obstacles they face and how they deal with such obstacles all affect how teachers perceive themselves as professionals and how they position themselves in the classroom. This positioning influences teachers' instructional practices.

◆ Narrative Research in Language Teacher Identity

> A painful school experience embarrassed me and contributed to my feelings of inadequacy. When I was in 7th grade, my teacher made a comment that humiliated me. She said that a book report that I wrote resembled "China Town English." Because I could not make the transition from oral to written English (academic writing), my intelligence was being questioned. Since I did not know that academic writing is more complex and formal than spoken English, my academic writing and my speech were similar. Rather than being humiliated, what I needed was guidance and explicit instruction on the differences between spoken and written registers and when and how to use each. My teacher should have explained to me that colloquial speech is not appropriate in academic writing and that academic writing relies on more complex syntactic rules and a higher-level vocabulary. Writing was my Achilles' heel.

This quotation comes from an autobiographical narrative written by Quy Tran, a Vietnamese U.S. immigrant who eventually earned an MA in TESOL degree and who is now an ESL teacher. The quotation draws attention to several facts. First, the teacher's words marginalized not only Quy but also other immigrant students who were ELLs. Although Quy does not state it in his narrative, it seems clear that the teacher saw Quy, and likely the other language learners in her class, as "the other," or as Kubota and Lin (2009) state, the "inferior Other" (p. 5), a sentiment that would lead some to call the teacher's comments racist because her statement was "inferiorizing ethnic groups" (Anthias & Yuval-Davis, quoted in Kubota and Lin (2009, p. 5).

In 2000, I "timidly" integrated a new assignment in the TESL 570 Educational Sociolinguistics course that I teach in the MA TESOL program. The assignment asked students to write an autobiographical narrative that reflected on how issues of race and ethnicity, language status and cultural background, life experiences, and self-perceptions affected their own process of identity negotiation and construction.

As part of the narrative, the students were asked to include a section on the relationship between issues of identity and language teaching and learning.

The assignment quickly became one of the most powerful and successful professional activities in which my students and I have engaged over the last several years. In fact, it led to the development of our (the narrative authors' and my own) increased awareness about the relationship between identity and language teaching. It has also helped us to understand the strong relationship between a teacher's professional identity and the teacher's positionality in the classroom.

While narrative inquiry has been used in the field of educational research since the late 1980s (see the work by Connelly & Clandinin, 1990, 1999; Clandinin & Connelly, 1995, 2000; Clandinin, Pushor, & Orr, 2007), in the field of TESOL, the use of narrative research (more specifically, autobiographical writing, one of the sources of data in narrative inquiry) is much more recent (e.g., Belcher & Connor, 2002; Casanave & Schecter, 1997; Curtis & Romney, 2006; Johnson & Golombek, 2002; Nunan & Choi, 2010). According to Connelly and Clandinin (1990), the study of narrative:

> is the study of the ways humans experience the world. This general notion translates into the view that education is the construction and reconstruction of personal and social stories; teachers and learners are storytellers and characters in their own and other's stories. (p. 2)

Narrative inquiry challenges Western views of scientific research in which notions of data validity, reliability, and generalizability are paramount (Connelly & Clandinin, 1990). The value of narrative inquiry lies in the fact that when teachers inquire into their own personal and professional lives, they speak in their own voice; narrative inquiry is the tool, then, that teachers use to give a first-person account on how they construct knowledge (Johnson, 2006). In this view, teachers are the ones that construct knowledge, rather than being the ones who are the subject of research, since it is the teachers themselves who tell their own stories.

A good example of the power of the autobiographical narrative in TESOL is the book edited by Curtis and Romney (2006), which captured the complexities of the intersection between race and language. Other recent examples of research that relies on the use of the narrative as a research tool are the studies by Chang (2004), Choi (2007), Lu (2005), and Tsui (2007), which provide rich descriptions of how NNESTs construct a professional identity.

In *Narrating Their Lives,* narrative inquiry is used in two ways. First, the autobiographical narrative is the heuristic that teachers use to tell their own stories. In writing their autobiographies, the teachers place emphasis on understanding the extent to which their stories may affect their instructional practices. Second, narrative inquiry is used to move beyond the stories and analyze them to identify instructional practices that draw on the teachers' life and professional experiences.

◆ The Theoretical Grounding of the Autobiographical Narrative as an Assignment

As previously mentioned, in the early 2000s, I timidly experimented with the integration of the autobiographical narrative as one of the assignments in my TESL 570 Educational Sociolinguistics class. After retooling the assignment guidelines and expectations, the autobiographical narrative has become a course staple. The autobiographical narrative, as well as memoirs and life histories, are examples of narratives that focus on "big stories." Big stories are those that deal with "the grander narratives we tell ourselves, the big retrospectives elicited from interviews" (Watson, 2007, p. 371, as quoted in Vázquez, 2011, p. 537). While the big stories have become widely implemented in TESOL education programs (see discussions on the autobiographical narrative by Barkhuizen, 2011; Johnson & Golombek, 2011;

Pavlenko, 2003), one of the shortcomings is that the final product often gives the impression of being too clean, too "polished" (Watson's term, 2007, p. 372, as quoted in Vázquez, 2011, p. 538) in the sense that the authors' identity seems to be more stable than it actually is (Freeman, 2007, as cited in Vázquez, 2011).

On the other hand, the autobiographical narrative has what Johnson and Golombek (2011) call a "transformative power" (p. 486) since, as they well put it, the narrative is "a mediational tool . . . in fostering teacher professional development" (p. 486). I believe that, in part, it is because of this "transformative power" that the pre-service teachers with whom I work find the autobiographical narrative to be so powerful. In completing this task, rather than isolating, for example, the language teaching methodologies to which the pre-service teachers have been exposed and reflecting on their advantages and disadvantages, pre-service teachers are asked to reflect on their own language learning experiences in relation to the social, political, and cultural contexts in which the learning process has been embedded. In fact, the pre-service teachers' stories could not be understood without taking into account the situations, whether historical, social, political, or educational in which they are contextualized (Elbaz-Luwisch, 2007).

One of the immediate benefits of completing autobiographical narratives is that knowledge is constructed "from the bottom-up" (Canagarajah, 1996, p. 327). This means that rather than engaging pre-service teachers in a banking approach to knowledge construction (relying on the knowledge produced by so-called experts in the field and then asking pre-service teachers to learn what these people have to say about language learning), the pre-service teachers develop their own theories of practice by reflecting on their language learning and life experiences (a point made by Kumaravadivelu, 2001). Another benefit is that the reflection process allows pre-service teachers to see more clearly the connection between their language learning and life experiences and their instructional beliefs and practices (and non-practices). After these teachers have developed an awareness (or have enhanced their awareness) about the various factors that affect their beliefs and practices, they are in a position to make more informed decisions about their current or future instructional actions.

In Chapter 5, I return to the autobiographical narrative assignment and discuss how the assignment is integrated in my teaching.

◆ Mixing *I* and *They*

It is only natural that a book that features autobiographical narratives be written in the first person. However, it is not common in the field of TESOL to find books that mix the use of the first person *I* and the third person *it* or *they* (what Vandrick, 2009, calls a "hybrid genre," p. 10). In this book, the *I* is present when the teachers tell their personal stories in the autobiographical narratives and when I draw on teachers' stories to introduce the book chapters and the various sections in each chapter. In contrast, the *they* is present when I interpret the teachers' stories to uncover how the teachers' instructional practices are informed by their stories.

When I started working on this book in 2007, I was deeply conflicted by the fact that the book contained a heavy mix of *I*'s and *it* or *they*.[2] However, after several rewrites, I came to the conclusion that the mix of both persons has two clear purposes in this book: The *I* allows, you, the readers to access the individual teachers' stories in their own voices and the *they* allows readers to access my analysis of the stories.

◆ The Structure of the Book

The book consists of five chapters. Each chapter opens with a question and concludes with a reflection question to guide readers and to make the book user-friendly for potential pre-service and in-service

---

[2]To my relief and pleasant surprise, Vandrick's (2009) excellent book, titled *Interrogating Privilege: Reflections of a Second Language Educator*, integrates both voices, which made me feel confident in the decision to use mixed voices in this book.

programs. Chapters 1, 4, and 5 open with a teacher's story or a quotation from a teacher so as to humanize the research reviewed.

In the first chapter I use the first person to describe my own EFL learning experiences, and then, I interpret my experiences in the context of traditional SLA research and current thinking in the TESOL field.

The second and third chapters present six teachers' autobiographical narratives. The main challenge I faced in organizing the chapters was identifying a common thread among the teachers' lives. Chapter 2 presents the autobiographies of a teacher born in the Philippines (Veneza Angel Pablico, henceforth, Angel) and two teachers born in South Korea (Hee-Jin Kim and Jessie Chen). Their narratives were selected from several dozen others because they reflect a variety of experiences of teachers who are transnational and transcultural; that is, rather than living in one country for their whole lives, they shuttle between (or across) countries and cultures. This shuttling is reflective of current globalization processes, in which flows of people move in multiple directions (Pennycook, 2007). These teachers reject being placed in categories or boxes (e.g., being native or nonnative speakers of English, belonging in one or another cultural group). At the same time, these teachers' narratives reflect different life and professional experiences, and these experiences have contributed to an understanding of how language classrooms should be settings where their students' identities are affirmed.

In the first autobiographical narrative, Angel describes her journey growing up in a multilingual society like the Philippines and her move to the U.S., where she learned American English and African American Vernacular English (AAVE). In the narrative, she explains that because of her multilingual learning experiences, she rejects the term *nonnative speaker* and sees herself as a multicompetent speaker (to use Cook's 1999 term). Additionally, she argues that it is this positive self-perception that, at least in part, led her to view her students' first languages as a classroom resource. The second autobiographical narrative in the chapter, written by Hee-Jin Kim, reflects her experiences shuttling between South Korea and the U.S. and between South Korea and Germany. Hee-Jin argues that these types of shuttling experiences are becoming more common for people around the world and so it should not be surprising to find teaching professionals like her, who do not fit the stereotypical mold of the blond, blue-eyed native English-speaker. In her narrative, Hee-Jin challenges employers to move beyond dichotomous views of professionals (native English speakers and nonnative English speakers) since such views do not tell much about their preparation, qualifications, and experience. In the last autobiographical narrative, Jessie Chen also describes her experiences shuttling between and across countries. However, central to her autobiographical narrative is a painful incident that occurred when she was an 8th grade Korean immigrant in a rural town in Arizona. As she explains in her narrative, she was physically and verbally attacked by a classmate simply because she was Asian-looking. Jessie recalls this experience in detail and explains that this racist incident led her to decide to master the English language so she could defend herself from other similar incidents. In her narrative, she also explains that her cultural and linguistic fluidity has allowed her to become a better teacher since she can help her students understand the importance of being multicultural and multilingual.

Chapter 3 presents the autobiographical narratives of three white teachers who were born in an Inner Circle country like the United States. While one could argue that the fact that the three teachers are white automatically makes their professional journeys unproblematic, their stories will defy that assumption. In fact, in selecting the stories that would be part of this chapter, I intentionally identified narratives that reflected that being white does not necessarily mean that one is a speaker of standard English, that one will be automatically perceived to be a "legitimate" teacher, or that one can easily fit into a linguistic community. The topic of race has only been a recently addressed in the TESOL field (see Curtis & Romney, 2006; Kubota

& Lin, 2006, 2009). In fact, while much of this work has focused on racial minority students and professionals (rightly so because there has been limited work focusing on them), my intention in this chapter was to integrate the voices of white teachers, whose experiences have not received much attention.

The first autobiography in the chapter, written by Jeremy C. Kelly, describes his experiences growing up in the rural South of the United States, where he was a native speaker of Southern American English, a dialect that marked him as a cultural outsider when he moved to New York. In his narrative, Jeremy explains how this life experience led him to learn standard American English as a means to gain in-group status. However, learning this dialect was not unproblematic because it made Jeremy feel that he was giving up his original identity. Eventually, after years of struggle, Jeremy developed a sense of comfort about his use of multiple dialects and now draws on it when teaching English language learners. The second autobiographical narrative is written by Valerie J. Callet and makes reference to her initial guilt for not identifying with her students in terms of race, home language, or dialect. Valerie's guilt led her to question her ability to teach her students; however, after reading Peirce's (1995) seminal work, in which Martina, one of her study participants "claimed the right to speak" (p. 23), Valerie realized that to be an effective teacher, she needed to replace her negative professional identity with an identity as a strong and caring teacher. In fact, the notion of caring, which was new to me in the context of scholarly work, is central in Valerie's description of her pedagogical practices. As will be explained in her narrative, the notion of caring has received growing attention in the K–12 literature (see Gay, 2010, for example). This notion goes well beyond what could be considered a teacher's interest in his or her students' well-being. Caring, as discussed in scholarly work, involves having high expectations for students' performance, accompanied by the cognitive and emotional support needed to meet instructional goals. The third autobiographical narrative, written by Shannon Ladymon, describes the picture of a professional who looks like "the quintessential American" (to use her term), which has led others to view her as a monocultural and monolingual. However, Shannon is a multicultural and multilingual professional who understands that it is important to help learners develop the skills needed to take ownership of the English language and have access to and be accepted in the communities of their choice.

I should note that the six autobiographical narratives contained in this book were rewritten over the last few years. These narratives, much like other chapters in the book, went through a blind review and editing process typical of any publication. As I read and reread the narratives, it became clear that with the passing of time, the research presented in them had become dated. Therefore, I have added footnotes to make reference to more current research on the topics being addressed by the narrative writers.

In the fourth chapter, I return to the six autobiographies in order to identify and discuss the connections between the teachers' personal and professional identities and the actions that they take (and don't take) in the language classroom in order to answer the question given at the beginning of the Introduction. However, I also hope to address three broader questions: What can we learn about teaching from the teachers' autobiographies? Or, how do the teachers' lives and professional identities inform the strategies they use to construct their classrooms? How can readers draw on the ideas presented in this book to enhance their own classrooms?

The final chapter in this book discusses how narrative research can be used by individual teachers and by teacher preparation programs to promote teacher development and growth.

I hope that readers will find some of their experiences reflected in the stories in this book. I also hope that the book challenges and enhances readers' understandings about the relationship between identity and language teaching and learning. Enjoy the journey.

Reflection Question

How have the ideas presented in the chapter helped you to further understand how your personal and professional identities may affect your actions (or non-actions) in the classroom?

CHAPTER 1

From "The Sound of Music" to "the Sound of Silence" and Back: Language Learning, Teaching, and Identity

Think about the first time you were in a foreign or second language class. Was your experience a good one or a poor one? What happened (or didn't happen) to cause you to think that way?

This chapter describes my first experiences as an EFL learner and then analyzes those experiences by drawing on two different explanations: one provided by traditional SLA research and the other by poststructuralist views in SLA. I also discuss how my initial experiences have influenced my instructional practices as a teacher educator.

◆ A Language Learner's Story

Like many professionals born and raised in Expanding Circle (Kachru, 1992) environments, I studied English so that, as an adult, I would have access to a higher paying job. While my mother's motivation for putting me in an EFL institute in Buenos Aires was instrumental because it was practical in nature, my own motivation for studying

English was significantly more ambitious. At the age of 10, my parents took me to see the movie "The Sound of Music." Something magical happened to me that day. When the movie ended, I left the theater dancing and singing in English, believing that I was or could become Julie Andrews even though I did not know a word of English. Right then and there I fell in love with the English language and everything the language represented.

As a language learner, my initial classroom experience was not a successful one. On the first day of class, my teacher, who had an excellent reputation and was professionally prepared as an EFL teacher, asked students to listen to and repeat vocabulary terms from a picture dictionary. When it was my turn to repeat the word *desk,* I got nervous and said *deks.* My teacher looked at me, snapped his fingers (signaling that it was my turn to repeat the word, as was the practice in the audiolingual method), and asked me to repeat the word *desk* again. I became more nervous and said *deks* again. After the fourth time that I repeated the word incorrectly, the teacher moved on to the next student. My confidence as a language learner dropped immediately and I became silent in class—although cognitively involved in the classroom activities—the rest of the year. Silence was not typical for me; everyone's perceptions of me were that I was an excellent and hard-working student. But in that EFL class, my voice literally disappeared. Outside the classroom I was an active and strategic learner who listened to The Beatles and played their songs thousands of times, trying to decipher what they were saying as I sang along. I also sought opportunities to interact with people in English, although in those days the opportunities were very limited.

◆ Understanding My Language Learning Experience

My initial experience as a language learner can be explained in two different ways. The first explanation would draw on traditional views of SLA, which place the burden of learning on the language learner.

The second explanation draws, for the most part, on the seminal work by Bonny Norton Peirce (see Norton, 1997; Peirce, 1995; Norton, 2000), which supports the notion that the language learning process cannot be isolated from the world in which the language learner is immersed (a point that has also been made by researchers like Pennycook, 2001, and Norton & Toohey, 2001).

As explained by Norton, traditional views of SLA would look at my classroom experience in terms of individual factors. For example, my silence could have been attributed to personality factors (e.g., introverted or extroverted, inhibited or uninhibited). In my case, my teacher could have described me as being introverted due to my lack of participation. Given that my classroom participation was very limited, I could have been perceived as not seeking opportunities to practice the language, which resulted in less input and, in turn, resulted in fewer opportunities to learn the English language.

Traditional views of SLA could also explain my lack of participation in terms of another individual factor: anxiety. The literature identifies three different types of anxiety (*trait:* a personality characteristic; *state:* the apprehension experienced in response to a specific learning situation like taking a grammar test; and *situation-specific:* in response to a general situation like public speaking anxiety) (Ellis, 1994). Anxiety has also been described as being debilitative, causing the learner to "flee" (Ellis, 1994, p. 482) the task, or facilitative, causing the learner to work hard toward the completion of the task. In my case, I could have been perceived as suffering from debilitative anxiety, causing me to have a high affective filter and leading me to withdraw from participation in activities that involved oral production; at the same time, the high affective filter would not allow the input received to go through the filter.

Another characterization of me in the classroom could have been that I was adverse to taking risks or that I was not a good language learner. Research on the "good language learner" spearheaded by Rubin (1975) and Wenden and Rubin (1987), has shown that good language learners know what strategies to use, know when to use them and how to use them, and seek opportunities to interact with their peers.

Still another explanation for my lack of participation could have been lack of motivation, understood as "the directed effort individual learners make to learn the language" (Ellis, 1994, p. 509). Because I was silent in the classroom, it was not possible for my teacher to see any overt effort, leading him to believe that I was not motivated to learn English.

My actions in the classrooms could also be explained by drawing on the work on classroom interactional analysis (Spada & Fröhlich, 1995). This work would attempt to explain my experiences by analyzing how much my teacher and I talked, investigating the types of questions that my teacher asked and the answers I gave, and analyzing my teacher's error correction (in terms of amount and type of error correction), etc. However, as noted by Morita (2004), this type of research would have only been able to explain behaviors that were observable; therefore, this line of research would have had little to say about a student like me. More importantly, this line of research would not allow for the development of an understanding of the "students' views and intentions" (Morita, 2004, p. 575).

These explanations for my behaviors as a language learner are problematic on two counts. First, as argued by Peirce (1995; Norton, 1997) in her seminal study focusing on five immigrant women in Canada, they disregard the fact that I, the language learner, functioned within a language learning context—in this case, the classroom—and, within this context, there were relations of power that affected my interaction and participation. Second, traditional descriptions of language learners depict them in terms of dichotomies (motivated or unmotivated, extroverted or introverted, anxious or confident, etc.) and do not take into account the fact that language learners have a complex identity, which at times can be "contradictory" (Peirce, 1995, p. 26) and changes "across time and space"

(Peirce, 1995, p. 26).[1] This was exactly my case. While I understand now that I *chose* to remain silent in the classroom—as a form of resisting often categorized as being a "poor language learner"—outside the classroom, I enacted my agency and developed an identity as a competent language learner (which was significantly more congruent with my overall self-perceptions as a student). My contradictory actions defy the notion of the language learner being "unitary, fixed and ahistorical" (Peirce, 1995, p. 17) and challenge the idea that I was either motivated or unmotivated, anxious or confident, etc.

Another line of research on which one can draw to explain my silence in the classroom is the research that looks at the role of silence in the L2 classroom, although this research has mainly focused on L2 minority students participating in mainstream classrooms in K–12 settings (Duff, 2001, 2002), community college classrooms (Losey, 1995, 1997) and graduate programs (Morita, 2004). Central to this work is the notion that the students' silence cannot necessarily be equated to passivity (Morita, 2004); instead, silent students may still be cognitively involved in the tasks at hand. Additionally, as shown in Morita's groundbreaking study of Japanese female students enrolled in a graduate program, the construction of the one's identity is situated—that is, the students' identity construction can be understood only by analyzing the classroom in which they participate.

◆ Lessons Learned from the Story

It was not until I became a language teacher, more than 30 years ago that I began to notice that my many experiences as a language learner—as well as my experiences outside the classroom in com-

[1]I should note that Peirce's work does not focus on the formal classroom setting; however, her ideas about the learner's social identity as not being fixed and, at the same time, as being affected by relations of power are applicable to the classroom setting since the latter can replicate the unequal relations of power that can be observed outside the classroom (a point made by Peirce herself).

bination with my values, beliefs, professional knowledge, and factors such as my religion, gender, social class, the settings in which I functioned, the generation to which I belong, and the students with whom I work—inform my construction of the classrooms in which I function. In fact, my identity as a teacher educator can be explained, though in part, by my initial experiences as an EFL learner.

My initial experiences as an EFL learner have affected my beliefs about teaching and learning and have led me to construct classroom environments that are designed to purposefully avoid silencing students. Specifically, in all my classes, I work to create classroom conditions designed to promote (in contrast to require) full participation on the part of all students. To this end, I do several things. First, at the beginning of the term, I schedule individual meetings of five to ten minutes with all the students who are taking one of my classes for the first time. At these meetings, the students and I discuss their future professional goals and current professional concerns. When I notice that international or immigrant students do not participate in class as often as other students, during the meetings I discuss the important role they play in the classroom. Rather than seeing them as future teachers whose second language may be deficient (a term that I purposefully never use)[2], I tell them that they are sources of knowledge since they have a first-hand understanding of the language learning and cultural adaptation processes. On the other hand, I also tell these students that they should not feel obligated to participate and, instead, should participate when they feel ready to do so. I learned to do this when, after years of encouraging students to participate, one Asian international female student told me that she knew she was disappointing me because, in spite of my encouragement, she still did not actively participate in whole class discus-

[2]My rationale for not using the term is that I defy the notion that someone who knows two languages can be perceived to be deficient solely on the basis that he/she may not be equally proficient in the two languages.

sions. At that point, I realized that, contrary to what I intended to do, I was equating silence with lack of mental involvement. However, I should note that while I do not require student participation, I do strategize with students so that they participate if they want to do so. To this end, I ask students to prepare an idea they want to share as part of the review stage of my lesson. Then, in class, when students and I are engaged in a review activity, I make eye-contact with selected students in order to allow them to share the information they prepared. Central to this simple strategy is the notion that if students get to hear their own voices, they begin to see themselves as legitimate participants of the classroom community; as a result, little by little, students take bigger steps in their process of classroom participation.

Another strategy I use to create a community of learners in which every student has something to contribute is to integrate asynchronous web-based forum discussions to which only the students in my classes have access. This allows student participation on their own time and at their own pace (Kamhi-Stein, 2000). In my research, I have found that web-based forums tend to act as equalizers of student participation in the sense that diverse voices and perspectives are shared. This is not to say that web-based forums are neutral. In fact, they can replicate a traditional classroom participatory structure like the one in the Initiation, Response, Evaluation (IRE) structure (Mehan, 1982), in which the teacher is in control of turn taking as well as the topic of the conversation. I believe that the reason this structure is not replicated in the web-based forum discussions in my classes is because I purposefully avoid leading the discussions as a means of creating conditions in which it is the students who are the owners of the discussion.

The final strategy that I use in order to promote what I call "an equal opportunity to participate" is to manage the classroom floor through turn-taking. Specifically, rather than allowing the more vocal students to blurt out their answers or monopolize the floor, I ask all students to take a minute or so to reflect on the question at hand and then volunteer to answer it. Students are well aware that while everyone is welcome to respond, both their peers and I want to hear multiple voices and perspectives. Initially, my students find my strategy "amusing"; however, after analyzing it, they realize that by slowing the pace of the discussion, I am ensuring that all students are able to participate, if they choose to do so.

While there are other strategies that I implement in my classes, the ones described are designed to avoid silencing students in the way that I was silenced as a child. At the same time, the strategies described promote conditions in which all students are able to participate on their own time and at their own pace. A word of caution is in order. While I believe that teachers' identities contribute to their instructional practices, I do not believe there is such a thing as a one-to-one correspondence between one's identity and one's actions in the classroom. For example, the fact that a teacher grew up using two languages and is bilingual does not necessarily result in that teacher's belief that the L1 can be used as a classroom resource. Or, the fact that I felt I was being silenced because I was mispronouncing a word does not mean that I will never require student participation in the classroom.

◆ Conclusion as Beginning

My goal in writing this chapter was to use my own story to provide an accessible account of how my initial EFL learning experiences affect one of the ways in which I construct my classroom. The next two chapters feature autobiographical narratives written by language teachers who work with ELLs. These teachers come from a variety of backgrounds and have diverse life and professional experiences that, in turn, affect how they perceive themselves and how they are perceived by others as professionals in the TESOL field.

Reflection Question

To what extent, if any, are your initial experiences as a language learner similar to or different from my own? After reading the chapter, would you explain your language learning experiences in a similar or different way?

CHAPTER 2

Narrating One's Life: Autobiographies of Transnational Teachers from the Expanding Circle

How do you define a native speaker of a language? What about a nonnative speaker? Make lists of what you think are pros and cons of being a native-speaking ESL/EFL teacher and an ESL/EFL teacher who is not a native speaker. Which of the pros and cons are actually stereotypes or generalizations as opposed to legitimate benefits or concerns?

This chapter presents the autobiographical narratives of Veneza Angel Pablico, Hee-Jin Kim, and Jessie Chen. Jessie and Hee-Jin were born in South Korea, and Angel was born in the Philippines. These autobiographical narratives reflect the journeys of these teachers as they became multilingual and adapted to life in new cultures (for example, the cultures of the countries to which they immigrated) or to the societal expectations of the countries in which they had been born. The authors also problematize the relationship between race and language status, argue against categorizing and labeling teachers (e.g., "native speaker" and "nonnative speaker"), and challenge employers whose hiring criterion too often relies on the "blond, blue-eyed native-speaker myth."

From Outer Circle to Inner Circle Society: A Code-Switcher's Sociolinguistic Journey

VENEZA ANGEL PABLICO
Intensive English Program, California State University, Los Angeles

The issue of native English-speaking teachers versus nonnative English-speaking teachers was a stimulating topic of discussion in my sociolinguistics class when I was a graduate student in a master's program in TESOL. Most of my classmates were able to provide insightful and well-argued viewpoints. During the discussion, however, I was silenced and confronted by a burning dilemma—I did not know which category I belonged in: native or nonnative speaker of English. As simple as it sounds, the question "Are you a native speaker of English or a nonnative speaker of English?" haunted me for several days. I could not provide a simple yes or no answer as my linguistic background did not unfold in such clear-cut lines. I even asked my mother, my best friend, and a friend whom I had known since childhood. Unfortunately, they provided me with contradicting answers: "yes," "no," and "I don't know." The inconclusiveness of my query led me to ponder the course of my linguistic development. I have identified two major phases: growing up in a multilingual society and acquiring American English through acculturation. I will describe both phases, discuss their relationship to my evolving social and professional identities, with implications for teaching, and then attempt to answer the seemingly simple yet thought-provoking question, "Am I a native speaker or a nonnative speaker of English?"

Growing Up in a Multilingual Society

I was born in the Philippines, a multilingual society with more than 170 native dialects. During its colonial period (1521–1898), the *lingua franca* or "common language used by speakers of different language backgrounds" (Sridhar, 1996, p. 53) in the Philippines was Spanish. In 1898, the United States liberated the country from Spain, and English became its lingua franca. After the U.S. interim government (1905–1935) left and handed power to the Filipinos, former President Manuel L. Quezon proclaimed Tagalog, which was the dialect spoken in Manila (the capital), and English the official languages of the Philippines. Philippine society is a clear example of Ferguson's (1959) notion of *diglossia*, in this case involving the use of two different codes for different purposes or in different domains.[1] In this diglossic situation, English is equivalent to what Ferguson labeled *high*, whereas Tagalog is equivalent to *low*. The former is the language more often associated with elites and highly educated people. It is the language used in formal situations, government and official proceedings, news and media, and colleges or universities. Tagalog, on the other hand, is the language more often associated with blue-collar workers and is more commonly spoken in intimate and informal settings. (This diglossic situation sporadically changes. When I was in high school, Tagalog and English were converging into a pseudo-Creole code called *Taglish*, which was commonly used in almost all aspects of communication. Currently, there is an ongoing movement toward minimizing English and promoting the indigenous language, Tagalog, by the media.)

As a child, I was surrounded by Tagalog speakers. People at church and in my neighborhood all spoke Tagalog. However, my parents, along with some relatives and family friends, spoke to me in English during my early childhood. According to my mother, my first words were in English and before I started kindergarten, I spoke English and "Taglish." I asked my mother why they spoke to me in English instead of Tagalog, and she told me that she wanted me to grow up bilingual because she knew that someday we would immi-

[1]While Ferguson's (1959) notion of diglossia referred to the use of two different varieties of the same language for different functions, Fishman (1972) expanded the notion to refer to bilingual communities in which two languages play different societal functions. The case of the Philippines is reflective of Fishman's definition.

grate to the United States. In addition, at that time, she considered English a superior language to Tagalog since it was often perceived as the language of intellectuals and the upper class. Aside from my family's language input, I also watched American television programs and cartoons like *Sesame Street, The Smurfs, Transformers,* and so on. Thus, at an early stage, I was exposed to both English and Tagalog.

During my first week in kindergarten, I remember being called "Ms. English-Speaking" by my classmates. In fact, when my classmates called me "Ms. English-Speaking," they did so in a derisive, manner. To avoid marginalization, I began to communicate with them in Tagalog, particularly on the playground. In the meantime, my kindergarten teacher taught us in a natural way (implementing techniques that I have come to associate with the Natural Approach) in English and encouraged us to speak English in the classroom. We sang mostly English songs and recited rhymes and riddles in English. It was in kindergarten that I first learned the two separate functions of English and Tagalog by knowing when and where to appropriately use each code: English was the language used in formal contexts like the classroom, whereas Tagalog was used to communicate with one another in informal settings like the playground.

In the Philippine education system, English is not a foreign language option but a mandatory core subject that is taught daily in elementary school, high school, and college. In fact, the teaching medium in the majority of all local schools in Manila is English. In the private school that I attended from elementary to high school, most of the subjects were taught in English. The only subjects that were taught in Tagalog were Philippine history, home economics, and Filipino (the Filipino language). Sometimes social studies was taught in Tagalog, but for the most part, it was taught in English. So, from first grade on, I concurrently and continually received grammar instruction in both English and Tagalog. I learned the various parts of speech, verb tenses, conjugations, and even composition and literary terms.

In my high school, English language use was highly promoted and implemented. During my sophomore year, I remember having a teacher who fined us 50 centavos or 1 peso for not speaking English. We could get in trouble for speaking Tagalog in the classroom. Our English language instruction was not limited to grammar; we had to read English literary works like *Silas Marner, Jane Eyre, Uncle Tom's Cabin, The Scarlet Letter,* and *Les Misérables* (the abridged English version), and then write book reports that included summaries and critical analyses. We also had to deliver speeches, participate in debates, and act in mini-plays in English.

However, growing up as a bilingual in the Philippines, I also compartmentalized my use of Tagalog and English. I frequently *code-switched* or spoke Taglish with my friends and family. Whereas I used English primarily in formal settings like the classroom, I used Taglish in intimate settings with friends and relatives. Thus, I grew up in a multilingual environment that was reflective of Ferguson's (1959) notion of diglossia.

Acquiring American English Through Acculturation

After graduating from high school in Manila, I moved to Los Angeles, California, where I lived for about six months. When I arrived in Los Angeles, I was pretty confident that I would acculturate easily and quickly; my English was fluent, my accent was subtle, and I had seen enough American movies to familiarize myself with the culture. In addition, I had visited my grandparents and spent several summer vacations in California before I became a permanent resident in 1998. As I expected, I blended in so well with my mimicked valley-girl accent that people could not tell I was a recent immigrant, or in slang terms, a "fob" (fresh off the boat). However, when I went to college in Oklahoma, I stood out as a foreigner. In Oklahoma, I attended a Bible college that had fewer than fifteen minority students, five of whom were international students. Out of these fifteen minority students, five were African-Americans from the Southern United States, three were Hispanics from Texas, or "Tejanos," three or four were international students from Kenya, and I was one of two Asians; the other Asian woman was an international student from Japan. Also, to my surprise, I was bombarded with regional idiomatic expressions like *fixing to, ya'll, I reckon,* and others that were all new to my foreign ear. I was laughed at and told that I spoke "like a book," which meant that I spoke too formally. I said things like *I purchased my books yesterday,* instead of saying, *I bought my books yesterday,* or *I submitted my homework,* instead of *I turned in my homework.* From then on, I made it a point to learn American colloquialisms, regionalisms, slang, and also when or where to use informal expressions as opposed to more formal vocabulary.

After living in Oklahoma for five years, I significantly improved my pragmatic competence in American English through acculturation (Schumman, 1978). That is, I adapted to the local culture through a process of cultural integration, or to put it in stronger terms, cultural immersion. For example, I stopped eating rice with every meal, learned how to make green bean casserole and deviled eggs, and acquired a taste for pumpkin pie and Dr. Pepper. As noted by Schumann (1978), individuals who feel close to the target language speech community and participate in it will better acculturate and therefore be more successful in their second language learning. By contrast, individuals who feel alienated from that community will tend to develop an L2 that is more pidgin-like (Schumann, 1978). This theory is apparent in my linguistic development. During my five-year stay in Oklahoma, while I integrated into the local culture, my access to Filipino culture was very limited. I met and became friends with only two Filipinos who could speak Tagalog. Thus, my use of Tagalog was limited to occasional meetings with them and infrequent phone conversations with my parents. By contrast, I have a few high school friends who also immigrated in the United States around the same time that I did, but they moved into Filipino-concentrated neighborhoods in San Francisco and Los Angeles. When I saw them after graduating from college, I noticed a difference in our accents and speech patterns. If I had not gone to Oklahoma to attend college my speech patterns and social identity would most likely differ significantly from what I have or am today.

My Evolving Social Identity

As I have traveled across the United States, my race and ethnicity have often piqued the curiosity of people I have encountered. Before disclosing information about my background, I ask them to guess and am sometimes amused by their responses. For example, in Oklahoma, I was frequently mistaken for a Latina. In New Mexico, someone asked me to which Native American tribe I belonged. In Arkansas, a church congregation thought I was from China or Vietnam. In Missouri someone told me, "You look mixed. You have black in you, huh?" When I first started teaching at California State University, Los Angeles, some of my colleagues thought I was from India. In the ESL classroom, my East Asian students can always tell that I am of Asian descent, but my Armenian, Persian, Arab, and Mongolian students sometimes assume that I am Mexican.

When I first started teaching, I expected to be easily perceived as a nonnative speaker of English because of my non-white features and perhaps because of my accent. I was apprehensive about whether my students would be open-minded to a female minority immigrant English teacher. Fortunately, I have not experienced racial discrimination from my students (at least to my knowledge). Most of them have been open-minded and respectful. I think the reason behind this is perhaps because I teach in Los Angeles, an ethnically diverse metropolis. Another possible reason is the cultural diversity in my work environment. I work with an ethnically diverse team of teaching professionals. Some of my colleagues have backgrounds similar to mine. I am just fortunate and grateful that I have not been victim of racial discrimination at my workplace (again, at least to my knowledge).

As I have moved to different places and spent time with people of various dialects, I have noticed that my accent evolves. My mother and cousin once told me that I acquired a "black accent" when I had been spending a lot of time with my African-American best friend. I am not sure what they meant by black accent. It could be that I had picked up a little bit of African American Vernacular English (AAVE) intonation or simply used expressions that they associate with AAVE. My boss, dentist, and uncle all once told me that I spoke with a midwestern or Oklahoma accent. But in Oklahoma, some of my classmates and roommates told me that I sounded like a Californian. Some people even identified me as having a foreign accent. Sometimes, out of curiosity and fun, I randomly ask people if they can hear a foreign accent in my speech. Some people say, "Yes, but it's very subtle," whereas others say, "No, you sound like you're from here." In the ESL classroom, most of my students cannot distinguish the regional varieties of American English nor other Inner Circle (Kachru & Nelson, 1996) varieties (e.g., British English from Australian English or Scottish from British). My students simply perceive me as someone who speaks English fluently.

To my students, what is most intriguing is my age. They have continually and suspiciously asked about my age. One of my older students actually questioned my supervisor about my teaching credibility because of my age. Most of my students at that time were Japanese, and their cultural image of a teacher or "sen-sei" is usually an older and therefore wiser person. This particular student had difficulty accepting that a 22-year-old teacher could be old enough and therefore credible enough to teach an adult ESL class.

Age discrimination is something that I still struggle with in my current employment. I get skeptical stares from students when I first walk in to the classroom and am often asked if I am the teacher when I ask for supplies or technical assistance in my classroom. One student even told me that I was too young to teach college. I, of course, disagreed with her and explained to her that credentials, experience, and the passion to teach are the most important factors for defining a good teacher, not age. Nevertheless, I have discovered that my age can be an advantage to students who are close to my age. Many of them see me as a good source of information about American pop culture, places to go in Los Angeles, slang, and other things that are of interest to them. Thus, some of my students can easily and comfortably relate to me because they perceive no generation gap between us.

Implications for Teaching

I have been teaching ESL for more than eleven years. I believe that my students' concern about my age will soon cease to be an issue. New challenges will arise and new factors will soon affect my social identity and career. So as I reflect on my experiences at this point of transition, I see a number of implications that may be of use to other teachers in the TESOL field.

Incorporate International Varieties of English

It is generally assumed that monolingual native speakers who were born in an Inner Circle (Kachru & Nelson, 1996) country (e.g., United States, England, Australia) are intrinsically better teachers or ultimate authorities of the English language. However, an increasing number of TESOL specialists now argue that nonnative, bilingual, and/or multilingual English teachers are extremely valuable to English language teaching. Matsuda (2003a, 2003b) advocated for the awareness of English varieties in English language teaching.[2]

---

[2]A more recent volume by Kachru and Smith (2008), focusing on the different varieties of English around the world, is designed to do exactly what Matsuda (2003a, 200b) proposed: promote "awareness and sensitivity to the formal and functional variation in Englishes" (p. xiv). A second volume, edited by Matsuda (2012), provides examples of how teachers from diverse countries like Japan, Turkey, and Inner Circle countries like Australia (for example) integrate instruction that, rather than imposing a particular variety of English, develop curriculum designed to prepare students to use English in international contexts.

Specifically, she suggested that "students should have more personal contact with people from other cultures, especially non-U.S./European" (2003a, p. 494) and that the integration of World Englishes into the curriculum can better prepare students for the use of English as an international language (2003b). I work with a culturally diverse team of teaching professionals. Some are nonnative English speakers born and raised in Expanding Circle (Kachru & Nelson, 1996) countries; some are multilinguals born and raised in the United States; and some are bilingual immigrants like me. My current workplace has had teachers from Scotland, South Africa, Mongolia, Vietnam, South Korea, Mexico, and the Philippines. This language learning environment not only exposes students to various cultures but also to international varieties of English.

When I tell my students that I am a Filipino immigrant, some of them automatically assume that I came to this country at an early age and grew up the United States. However, when I tell them that I came to the United State at the age of 16, I get reactions of surprise and more questions. The conversation then typically turns into a discussion of bilingualism, multicompetence, societal multilingualism, and English varieties. I tell them about my upbringing and explain the idea of multicompetence, which Cook (n.d., Evidence for Multicompetence) defines as "knowledge of two or more languages in the same mind." Furthermore, I tell them about bilingual education and that English is an official language of the Philippines. By the end of the discussion, my students become aware of Outer Circle (Kachru & Nelson, 1996) varieties of English like Filipino English, Singaporean English, and Indian English. This awareness is important so that they can develop an understanding of the different varieties of English that exist around the world.

One of my former students once mentioned that he preferred nonnative speakers as teachers because his best grammar teacher was a nonnative speaker. He also explained that nonnative English–speaking teachers were less intimidating than their native English–speaking colleagues. This anecdote echoes Cook's (1999) notion that language teaching would benefit from including teachers in the role of L2 users. According to Cook (1999):

> an interesting type of L2 user role is the nonnative-speaker teacher . . . students may feel overwhelmed by native-speaker teachers who have achieved a perfection that is out of the students' reach... Students may prefer the fallible nonnative-speaker teacher who presents a more achievable model." (p. 200)

The roles of nonnative, bilingual, and/or multilingual teachers from Outer Circle and Expanding Circle countries (e.g., Japan, South Korea, Armenia) are valuable in helping students become flexible and successful L2 users because English is an international language.

Select Materials that Include Successful L2 Users

Experts in the TESOL field have condemned Americentrism and Eurocentrism in language teaching and materials development (Amin, 2004; Cook, 1999; Kamhi-Stein, 1999; Matsuda, 2003b). Instead, they encourage teaching professionals to present internationally acceptable versions of the target language in the ESL classroom (Amin, 2004; Matsuda, 2012). In my workplace, I am responsible for selecting the textbooks for my classes. One of the criteria for evaluating and selecting an appropriate course book is that it must include L2 users portrayed as intelligible and successful participants in the target language community. Many publishers and course materials in ESL settings now feature international students as competent L2 users in tertiary academic institutions. According to Cook (1999), L2 users "should be considered as speakers in their own right, not as approximations to monolingual native speakers" (p. 185). Thus, course books should represent students positively so that they have successful models to emulate, rather than deeming themselves hopeless, fossilized nonnative speakers (a point made by Cook in reference to L2 users).

Look at the Students' First Language (L1) as a Resource

When I was hired to teach ESL at a community college, I was given one of my colleague's course syllabi to serve as a model for me to develop my own. Under classroom policy in that syllabus, I read "English will be the only language used in class!" all in capital letters with an exclamation mark. Upon reading this, I had a sudden flashback of my high school teacher who punished us for speaking Tagalog in the class by fining us 50 centavos or 1 peso. This traditional view has been widely opposed by many TESOL professionals and supporters of bilingual education. Auerbach (1993), for instance, found that "the rationale used to justify this English-only policy is neither conclusive nor pedagogically sound" (p. 9). She further argued that "L1 and/or bilingual options are not only effective but necessary for adult ESL students with limited L1 literacy or schooling . . ."(p. 9). As an adult ESL instructor, I agree with this argument because I have encountered students in such situations. In my Level 1, or beginning-level class, I have had students who were high school dropouts or had limited education in their country. For these students, I can see the necessity of the L1, particularly when presenting meaning. Much of the time, these particular students do not understand what is happening in class or how to complete the assignments because of their very limited vocabulary. As a result, they have had to rely on the translations of other classmates who spoke the same language or refer to their bilingual dictionary if they had one. If I prohibited such consultation or translation and enforced the English-only policy, how would these students be able to do the tasks and, therefore, succeed in my class? Sometimes students cannot convey their questions, problems, or ideas to me in the target language, so they consult another classmate or use a bilingual dictionary. If I restricted this practice and once again enforced the English-only policy, how could I help them? Would this be effective teaching?

I admit that in certain circumstances, I do enforce the English-only policy. For instance, if a particular group of students who share an L1 dominate the class or create an in-group, making others feel uncomfortable or alienated by constantly and only speaking to one another in their L1, then I enforce English-only in order to keep the class on track. However, we should not have a zero tolerance attitude toward L1 usage in the classroom since it can be a valuable resource for students with limited English proficiency. Instead, we should acknowledge the role that the L1 can play in learning the L2 by allowing students to use bilingual dictionaries and/or consult their classmates.[3]

The term *native speaker* has traditionally been defined as "someone who learned a language in a natural setting from childhood as first or sole language" (Kachru & Nelson, 1996, p. 81). However, recent work in the field of TESOL/applied linguistics has challenged the validity of the native speaker construct (see Braine, 2010; Kamhi-Stein, 2014, for a summary of the research on the topic). In my opinion, the polarized labels—native and nonnative—are too limiting. How do we account for people who speak Outer Circle varieties or for those with linguistic backgrounds similar to mine? I acquired English in a natural setting from childhood; however, it was not my sole language. In the TESOL field, this issue needs to be further investigated. When I see job advertisements for teaching positions that hire only native speakers, I am once again confronted with the dilemma. The native/nonnative labels should not be the basis for hiring because, as Liu (2004) puts it, "the success of TESOL professionals does not depend on whether they are native speakers or nonnative speakers" (p. 37). Rather, it depends on other significant factors such as education, preparation, training, experience, passion, and motivation (Liu, 2004).

Finally, how do I answer the question, "Are you a native speaker or a nonnative speaker of English?" Well, my answer is that I am nei-

[3]A book by Levine (2011) illustrates how the L1 can be strategically used in the L2 classroom.

ther one. How do I perceive myself? I perceive myself as a bilingual or a multicompetent speaker. I learned English and Tagalog at the same time, and I have been code-switching ever since I can remember. My fluency in these two languages has made me flexible, powerful, and skillful in responding to all of life's demands. As an immigrant to this country, I have managed to survive and adjust culturally by communicating effectively in English. The same ability also helped me to succeed academically. Although I have acculturated to the United States successfully, continuing to communicate in Tagalog with my family has prevented me from completely assimilating into the dominant culture, enabled me to preserve some of my Filipino culture, and allowed me to develop a blended cultural identity.

Learning to Fit In and Create My Own Place

HEE-JIN KIM
California State University, San Marcos

Once at a job interview for an EFL teaching position in Seoul, Korea, an employer told me he did not know how to categorize me. "You sound like an American, yet you are a Korean. You don't sound like a Korean, but you can't be a Korean-American because you're not a U.S. citizen. And to make matters worse, you don't hold a degree from a U.S. university," he said. I wondered why such categorizing was necessary when all I wanted was a job. Apparently, one was not available, at least not for me. There were several explanations for my problem. First, there is some evidence most employers prefer to hire native speakers as teachers (Cook, 1999; Liu, 1999).[4] Korean employers seem prefer to hire white North Americans, which I clearly was

---

[4]Research by Clark and Paran (2007) and Selvi (2010) further confirms the notion that employers favor hiring native English speakers. However, the employers' idea of who is a native speaker is rather problematic since it may rely on factors such as an applicant's place of birth or country issuing a passport.

not. Second, Korean employers, language experts, and learners expect that, to be fully qualified as a nonnative English-speaking teacher, a person needs to have majored in either English literature or linguistics. My major was German Education with a minor in English. At the university I graduated from, German Education was a major in the College of Education. Acquiring credits toward a teaching credential was part of the graduation requirements, and since I minored in English, my teaching credential was good for teaching both English and German at secondary schools. However, even though I was eligible to teach the two languages, this was not considered sufficient in Korea. Moreover, it seemed to me at that time that employers tended to hire language instructors who had graduated from U.S. universities or colleges. At that time, I had not attended any institution in the United States. This job interview happened long before I started my graduate program at California State University, Los Angeles, and became familiar with the issues of nonnative English-speaking teachers (Hansen, 2004; Liu, 2004; Medgyes, 1992; Prodromou, 1992).

As my experience shows, labeling is common, if not inevitable, especially in places like Korea where people tend to hold strong stereotypes of what an English instructor should look like. Arguing for or against the appropriateness of labeling is fruitless because labels will always exist. I identify as a NNEST because that label gives me a clearer sense of how I currently see myself and my place in the world, but I believe that when labels are the only criteria used to evaluate teachers and their teaching skills and ability, they are problematic because they limit both the teacher's and the learner's opportunities. I would like to use this narrative to illustrate how my linguistic and social identity has changed and how this identity affects my teaching in the classroom. Additionally, I would like to extend the implications of my experiences as an ESL student, EFL student, and EFL instructor to future NNESTs who, like myself, are beginning to establish a new demographic of English teachers. Ultimately, I hope to show that NNESTs make a uniquely valuable contribution to the classroom and that the NNEST label itself is a marker of this distinction.

Identity Confusion

In 1983, when I was six years old, my family and I moved to the United States so that my father could pursue his doctorate in electrical engineering at the University of Texas at Austin. My younger brother and I were too young to understand what it meant to move to another country where everything and everyone was different from where we were born and raised. We could not foresee how it would change our lives and so we were more excited than worried. When it was time for me to start my first day of first grade in Austin, I was slightly better off than Hansen (2004). Hansen, who was born in Denmark and moved to the United States, entered school with an English vocabulary of three words: *yes, no,* and *love*. I had mastered four words: *yes, no, apple,* and *teacher*, so I was very confident. My mother, however, did not seem to share my self-assurance because she handed me a piece of paper with my home phone number and instructed me to say the words *Help me* and show the paper if I needed anything, so that whoever was helping me could get in contact with my parents. When I arrived in the classroom, I was assigned a seat next to another Korean girl who was my translator for a good amount of time. However, my four vocabulary words and my translator were not enough for me to stay in regular classes, so I was sent to an ESL teacher during reading classes. I cannot recall exactly how many hours I spent there, but I worked with her for the entire first grade.

After my first year in a U.S. school, I was able to communicate in English. After living in the United States for almost six years, I was fluent in English as though it were my native language. On the other hand, I had forgotten a great deal of my native language, Korean, because I rarely spoke it. At home, my parents always spoke to me and my brother in Korean because that was the language they were most comfortable with, but it was fine for us to respond to them in halting Korean or even in English. My brother and I communicated with each other in English. And the moment I stepped out of my house, I used only English. As a result, I felt more comfortable in English, and I could express my thoughts more accurately in English. Another reason I avoided speaking Korean outside my home was that it made me different from my U.S. classmates. This difference made me very uncomfortable because I was often made fun of or looked at with surprise when I spoke Korean in front of other children. I already looked different, and that was enough for me. Although I never identified myself as an American, I did not want to be identified as "non-American" either.

After almost six years in Austin, my father completed his degree, and my family was ready to return to Korea. We moved to Daejeon, at that time a small city that the Korean government was developing into a high-tech community—similar to the Silicon Valley in Northern California—because my father's company had relocated there. Returning to Korea, my feelings were just the opposite of those I had when I started school in the U.S.: I was more worried than excited. Although Korea was where I had been born and raised until the age of six, it could not have been more foreign to me. I could not speak Korean fluently, and I could not read or write it at all. In the summer of 1988, I was in a new environment surrounded by people who all looked like me, and yet I did not feel like one of them. I was not sure who I was. One episode stands out in my memory and illustrates my confusion well. While I was watching the 1988 Seoul Olympics just after I had returned to Korea, I did not know whom to root for. I cheered for U.S. victories but felt guilty about it at the same time. I sang "the Star Spangled Banner" after every U.S. gold medal, but I found myself longing to hear the national anthem of Korea and see the Korean flag high in the air.

I was enrolled in middle school when I returned to Korea, and it did not take long for the word to spread that there was a new girl from the U.S. in school. Soon after, I was labeled "the American girl who doesn't know how to speak Korean." My classmates did not use this label to hurt me; to them, I was exotic and it was more like a nickname to them. As mentioned, when my family moved to Daejeon, it was an undeveloped city with a large population of low-income families. None of my classmates had ever been to the United States, and they had only recently begun to study English. It was not until 1997 that the Korean government made English mandatory in public elementary schools, beginning in third grade (Jung & Norton, 2002). Currently, however, children are exposed to English before they even go to elementary school because their parents believe that early exposure will facilitate their English acquisition and give them an advantage over other children. It was not surprising then that my classmates found me interesting. They were all eager to ask me questions about my life in the U.S. and hear me speak this different language.

This curiosity about the new girl, however, did not lead to new friendships. It was hard for me to make friends because of the language barrier and my lack of cultural understanding. At first I did not mind my nickname, but eventually, I came to dislike it because it reinforced my difference. I did not like standing out any more in Korea than I had in Texas. I worked hard to learn Korean, catch up with my peers, and overcome my difference. I wanted to fit in, so I learned the games Korean kids played and the songs they sang. I did not play the games purely for entertainment, nor was I singing the hip songs because I liked them—they were part of a conscious and strategic attempt to fit in. At the same time, I would cry every night, asking my parents to send me back "home." I now know how heartbreaking it was for my parents to see me go through this difficult period, but at the time, they would only tell me that this was home now and that I would have to work hard and try my best to accept my circumstances. To help me, they acted as tutors. Every day, I practiced reading, writing, and speaking Korean with them. We did homework together, and my mother would preview the next day's material with me so that I would be able to follow the class. Although I thank them now for providing me with a childhood that cultivated an understanding of two cultures—something that greatly benefits me as an EFL teacher—this was a hard time for me and for my whole family.

Nonetheless, life went on, and I reached a level of Korean proficiency where nobody was able to detect that I had ever lived abroad. I made sure that I did not overtly disclose this secret. I "de-accented" my English and in fact tried to use as little English as possible. After this assimilation process, I enrolled in college. Everyone who knew about my time in the U.S. expected me to major in English because people believed I had such a high level of English proficiency. Yet I chose to major in German Education with an English minor. After my sophomore year, I traveled to Wuerzburg, Germany, to study at a university as an exchange student. Learning German gave me great satisfaction. Not only did I improve my language skills, but I also had the opportunity to engage in the formal study of a language as a second language—unlike my acquisition of English, a language in which I been immersed from an early age in an ESL setting. I did not have the advantage with German that most of my Korean classmates thought I had had with English in middle and high school. I felt less guilty recalling how easy English classes were for me then; learning German, I was on equal footing with most second language learners, and I could even envy the few who had near-native proficiency in German. I returned to Seoul in 1999 to complete my studies and graduate. After one year in Germany, my German was proficient enough for me to consider becoming a translator in English, German, and Korean. Finding a job with my teacher's credentials was the last thing I was looking for.

After graduation, I obtained a job as a translator for a newspaper company, but I resigned after a year. It was not what I had imagined; it was not fulfilling. I took some time off to look for a different job, and to support myself, I decided to temporarily teach English to Korean professionals. While I had never felt any desire to be a teacher, little by little, I found myself wanting to teach more classes. I enjoyed meeting students who wanted to learn from me. I felt fortunate to work with people who appreciated my style of teaching. I felt like I could use my English abilities without the stigma that I had to deal with when I was in middle and high school. I did not know that I would find pleasure teaching others English and that my experience learning German would help me teach English. It was rewarding to know I had helped students improve. It was at this point that I knew that teaching was the career I wanted to pursue, so I began to look into this field more seriously.

But Then, Confused Again

When I was young and first returned to Korea from the United States, I eventually assimilated to the Korean culture, and my identity on some level was a given—it was not, for a while, something I pondered: I was a Korean citizen to begin with, I was living in Korea where my physical appearance did not stand out, and most importantly, I came to feel Korean at heart. From time to time, I would briefly imagine what life would have been like if my family and I had stayed and lived in the United States, but over the years I had completely transformed into a Korean.

However, my uncertainty about my identity surfaced again when I considered teaching English as a career. Although I did not then and never have identified myself as a native English speaker (NES), I found that professionally I was different from the typical NNEST in Korea because of my U.S. accent, my experience abroad, and my training as an English teacher. However, despite these advantages and despite the joy of interacting with students, I quickly discovered that finding a job in the Korean market was a nightmare for me. Employers could not see beyond my physical appearance, and my fluency in Korean caused them automatically to label me as a NNEST. Soon, it became my only label. Some employers told me they doubted how much English I would remember because I had been in the United States so long ago. Moreover, I found that Korean employers showed preference for white North Americans. The same people who would not hire me because of my Asian appearance and my language skills in Korean hired monolingual and less-qualified, but white, North Americans. I have worked with NES instructors who did not have any type of teacher training but were hired solely because English was their native language. Even more discouraging, employers often seemed to hire white Europeans who were also NNESTs just because they looked the part.

As Liu (1999) points out, NNESTs are at a disadvantage in the job market because of the preference for NES instructors (see research by Clark & Paran, 2007; Selvi, 2010), and many NNESTs "try to minimize their identity as nonnative speakers," (p. 98) by taking on an English name, for example. This was no different for me: I was required to use my English name, *Helen,* in some language schools I worked for, or even pretend I could not speak Korean at all. Even though I am fluent in English, I am not a North American, and to claim that I am amounts to a denial of my identity. In spite of my personal identity as a nonnative English–speaking Korean, I do not identify wholly as a NNEST.

I realized during this time that I needed to resolve, or at least find a way to accommodate, this duality. So, from shortly thereafter on, I made my ethnicity clear in every interview and indicated on every resume I sent out that I was a NNEST. At the same time, my resume emphasized my stay in the United States, my job as a translator, and my teaching credentials as indications of my experience, qualifications, and knowledge. Apparently, emphasizing these qualities was still not enough for the employers because I was rejected. If I was offered a job, it was to teach lower-level conversation or test-preparation classes where students were well informed of the fact that I was Korean and where Korean teachers taught English through Korean. For example, the very first school for which I worked had me teach a Level 1 conversation class for more than a year. In another school where I applied for a teaching position, an administrator very honestly told me that their policy was to only hire native speakers since that was what their students demanded. As a result, I became frustrated during interviews and struggled with self-doubt afterward. I wanted to be proactive but did not know how to begin. I even questioned whether I had made a smart career choice. All doors seemed to be closed to me.

It was as if society wanted me to have exactly the opposite identity of the one I had. When I was a child in the United States and was labeled Korean, I tried to act like one of the North American girls, but could never really be one. When I finally labeled myself as a Korean after successfully assimilating into the Korean community, I was asked to act like a North American. I was more discouraged than hopeful and even reached a point where I felt like the entire

English-teaching endeavor would be impossible for me. However, I persevered, and eventually I found employers who did welcome my complex label: a nonnative English–speaking Korean female with a U.S. accent who studied German. I did not have to take on my English name; I did not have to pretend I could not understand or speak Korean; and I did not have to hide the fact that I had studied German.

Problematic Dichotomies and Problematic Hiring Practices

As long as the terms *native speaker* and *nonnative speaker* exist in the field of TESOL, teachers will be categorized as one or the other. To me, the terms do not connote greater or lesser teaching ability; in fact, it has been shown that both groups of teachers serve different but similarly valuable purposes (Liu, 1999; Mahboob, 2004; Pasternak & Bailey, 2004). Therefore, the best and most effective language institutions will have a good balance of teachers from both categories to complement each other in a way that provides the maximum benefit to students (Medgyes, 1992). However, Korean employers, much like employers in other Expanding Circle (Kachru, 1992) countries, need to consider the fact that, in the future, more instructors will have experiences similar to mine. More contemporary families are able to provide opportunities for their children to live in an English-speaking country for an extended period of time—mostly the United States—for the sake of English language acquisition. Therefore, it is becoming more common to see children who have native-like English pronunciation and proficiency. Employers and learners alike will need to look beyond the dichotomy of native versus nonnative speakers as teachers, because soon in Korea, and in other countries, there will be many instructors who are facing issues similar to the ones I have described. And if these instructors are not hired just because they do not fit the employers' outdated and increasingly irrelevant definition of a *native speaker* of English, it will significantly disadvantage Korea's English education.

What I Bring to My Classrooms

As a NNEST who acquired English in a natural setting but who also had the experience of learning a foreign language, I believe my contributions are unique. I always start the first day of every class with a personal introduction. I briefly relate my childhood experience abroad and the struggles I faced after I came back from the United States. Many students have told me that hearing my story is motivating. Phillipson (1994) points out that the ideal instructor in the European foreign language teaching setting is not a native speaker but a nonnative speaker who has gone through the process of learning the language that he or she is teaching.

I see myself as an as amalgam of what Medgyes (1992) describes as the ideal NES instructor and the ideal NNEST: the ideal NES instructor is someone who has a high degree of proficiency in the learners' L1, and the ideal NNEST is someone who has acquired a near-native-like proficiency in English. As an instructor, I am able to offer a combination of these qualities, as well as an in-depth knowledge of both Korean and U.S. culture. Of particular benefit to my students is the fact that I am able to point out the similarities and differences between the two languages since I have command of both. Additionally, because I have a U.S. accent, I am often hired to teach conversational English classes. In those classes, many students want to improve their pronunciation. From my experience, I have observed that language learners tend to produce unfamiliar English sounds by approximating sounds that exist in their native language. One instance is the variation of the English vowel *o*, which is typically phonetically transcribed as /ɑ/ (a low, backed, non-rounded vowel) in standard American English. For American English speakers, this letter is used to capture a variety of sounds, as in words like *shopping* and *go*, which differ in pronunciation (/ɑ/ and /ow/, respectively). Many Koreans tend to pronounce the English /ɑ/ like the Korean vowel /오/, which sounds more like the non-rounded /ow/ in *go*. Therefore, their *shopping* sounds somewhat like /show-ping/. It is often easier for them to conceptualize how a certain sound is made by the subtle differences I explicitly point out, using both English and Korean phonology, rather than just having them repeat after a native English speaker. Improvement in pronunciation seems to be very important to students and is one of the ways they benchmark their overall progress. I see an instant boost of confidence when they understand subtle phonological differences and are able to correct themselves.[5]

I am also able to explain why some of the expressions they use do not make sense in the English context because it is easy for me to detect why they constructed a phrase the way they did. One student, for example, approached me after class and said, *Thank you for your hard work you put in for this class.* Interestingly, one of my NES colleagues had heard a similar construction and, thinking it odd, had mentioned it to me. In Korean culture, it is polite to say *thanks for all the hard work you put in for this class* to the teacher after class. So the student was translating word for word. Had I not spoken Korean or been knowledgeable about Korean customs, I would not have known what he was trying to convey, just like my colleague did not. However, because I speak Korean, I knew exactly what he meant and why he was saying it, and I was able to explain the difference, both syntactically and culturally, to the student (and to my colleague).

Although the TESOL field is divided on whether to use the students' L1 in the classroom, I have always benefited from using Korean with Korean-speaking students, either in the classroom or outside the classroom, when students come to me individually with questions. However, I use the two languages strategically, and for different pur-

[5]I should note that current thinking in the TESOL field emphasizes the importance of helping students become intelligible rather than sounding exactly like native speakers. This change in emphasis removes the burden of trying to sound like some idealized speaker (see Burns, 2005, cited in Kamhi-Stein, 2014). Additionally, recent research on accent has shown that teacher "accentedness" is independent of intelligibility (Butler, 2007; Kim, 2008); that is, a teacher's accent does not necessarily prevent students from understanding him or her. What a teacher's accent has been found to affect is students' perceptions of comprehensibility. This means that a teacher who is perceived to have a stronger accent is also perceived to be more difficult to understand (Kim, 2008). In turn, these perceptions lead students in EFL and ESL settings to have more positive attitudes toward teachers who sound more like a native speaker (Butler, 2007; Kim, 2008).

poses. I use Korean to explain a concept and to help my students understand and to reinforce a concept. For instance, in Korean, the present perfect tense does not exist. It is one of the hardest English grammar points for students to understand and use correctly. I use Korean in my initial explanation of what the present perfect is and how it differs from the simple past. Then I briefly explain it again in English, so that students can listen to the explanation in English without feeling overwhelmed. Since they understand most of the explanation, they feel that learning the present perfect is easier. They also feel a boost in their confidence in learning English because they understand more of what is being said. After this, I use English to help students practice and reinforce this new grammar lesson.

I have noticed that many language learners tend to rely on literal translation from one language to another when they are struggling to find the right word or expression. I try to stress that learning a new language is not just translating word for word. One of the examples I frequently use is the English expression *piece of cake.* There is a similar expression in Korean, but we express it using rice cake. Instead of saying that something easy is a *piece of cake,* we say it is *like lying down and eating rice cake.* I say to my students, "You would not say the test was like lying down and eating rice cake. Right?" Most students laugh, not because my example is particularly funny, but because they realize that they make similar mistakes. I encourage them to refer to Korean to evaluate similarities and differences between the two languages, but to never use Korean to produce English. Understanding conceptual and structural similarities and differences between languages, and when and how to use each, is beneficial in deepening students' understanding of both languages, and of language itself. I am able use my own command of both languages and cultures, as are all bilingual English instructors, to teach English.

I agree with Medgyes (1992) and Phillipson (1994) that the experience of an instructor who has undergone the complex process of learning English as a second or foreign language may be of more benefit to students than that of an instructor who acquired English in a natural setting. Some students will point out that I had it easy because

I was immersed in an English-speaking environment at a young age. They say I do not understand the difficulties of learning English in an EFL environment. I tell these students that I may not fully understand what learning English in an EFL environment is like, but that I have a similar experience in learning another language. I go on to share how I "attacked" German to become proficient.

Instead of offering them only simple phrases of encouragement like *you can do it* or *try harder,* I am able to give them concrete ideas, drawn from both my experience and my training, about to how to learn a foreign language. For example, one of my greatest obstacles to learning German was memorizing vocabulary words. I find my students have similar problems. Vocabulary flashcards were very helpful to me and so I show my students how to make flashcards, advise them on what kind of information to include, such as the meaning of the word and example sentences that show how the word is used in context, and the number of words they should try to learn daily.

I remind students that learning English is not a start-to-finish project but an ongoing process. Although I started to learn English in a natural setting, I was placed in an EFL setting after the age of 12. I point out to my students that I too had to "study" English in order to improve my English and better myself, something I do even today. I reveal that I have to consult the dictionary and that I practice speaking by reading out loud to become comfortable with unfamiliar expressions. I even show them notes I took on the way to class, new expressions or words I circled in the newspaper that I did not know. I am not ashamed to let them know that I consult my NES colleagues for help because, as I explain to them, I am still learning. Some teachers feel vulnerable showing their weaknesses, but I find that showing the time and effort I have invested in learning English encourages my students and also shows them that this is a necessary component of proficiency. It is important for my students to realize that language learning, besides being fun, is facilitated by consistent and strategic effort.

Still, being a NNEST remains a challenge on many levels. It is difficult, for example, to satisfy students who are resistant to the idea of a NNEST or who believe that NNESTs do not have as much to offer. I would like to note that I am aware and respectful of the importance of ESL/EFL teachers who are native English speakers and of the powerful impact they can have on students (Liu, 1999). My intention is not to downplay this contribution whatsoever. However, my strength, which is the strength of many nonnative English-speaking teachers, is my ability to relate to my students as a nonnative speaker with a unique language background, and to use this background to my students' advantage. I have much more to learn and explore, but I hope my experience thus far as a NNEST teacher will heighten awareness of teachers like me and of what we have to offer because this population will only continue to grow.

As a final thought, I would like to make it clear that while I believe that NES instructors and NNESTs are different (Medgyes, 1992); I also believe we need to see beyond the native/nonnative-speaker dichotomy. Just saying that someone is a native or a nonnative English-speaking teacher does not help understand much about that professional. For example, I am a NNEST. I fit the description that the literature presents of NNESTs. However, I am also a NNEST who speaks English with an U.S. accent and learned German much like my students learn English. The description that follows after my NNEST label is as important if not more. I believe I could have been a positive addition to the schools that rejected me not *in spite of* but *because of* my nonnativeness. Teachers should be able to take on classes that show their strengths, whether these stem from their native or nonnative speaking ability. I may not be the best candidate to teach certain aspects of U.S. culture—an instructor with a longer relationship with U.S. culture is more suited to teach this, but I am able to relate to my students and teach them in a way a NNEST cannot. Ultimately, I want to be "hired and evaluated" (Hansen, 2004, p. 55) according to my abilities and professional preparation and to use these abilities and preparation to contribute to the TESOL community.

A Culturally Amorphous ESL Teacher

JESSIE CHEN
Santee Education Complex, Los Angeles Unified School District

My Journey to Becoming a NNEST

Although I am a U.S. citizen and have lived in the United States since I was 11 years old, I am frequently asked, "Are you Korean?" I usually hesitate before I can say, "Yes, I am." I think I am, but then I know I am not, at least not entirely. As I have lived in three different countries (Korea, Taiwan, and the United States) and nine different cities and currently have residences in three cities (San Diego, Los Angeles, and Taipei), I feel that I am part of a transnational diaspora with not one, but many, cultural localities. If in the past the term *diaspora* was limited to race or ethnicity, primarily signifying the dispersed Jews, Blacks, and Armenians, Cohen (1997) argues that the word *diaspora* has transnational scope. It now includes all races of contemporary "traveling cultures" (Cohen, 1997), cultures that have lost their territorial moorings because of today's affordable and efficient means of communication and transportation. Similarly, Bhabha (1998) argues that one's location of cultural production is in an interstitial cultural space called "the space of beyond" where one's past and present conjoin in a pluralistic and complex reality (Bhabha, 1998). Drawing from Cohen's and Bhabha's theories, I believe that my multicultural subjectivity fits their model of postmodern diaspora, or what I call a "cultural hybridity," in that I am Korean by birth, American by law, Chinese by association, and all of the above and beyond geopolitically and socioculturally.

I have developed an indomitable sense of self, at least in part, at the price of racial discrimination, which I have tenaciously turned to my advantage. Growing up in the United States, my Asian appearance sometimes caused others to release the worst, belligerent energy in them, resulting in racial bigotry. Among the instances of racial injustices I have encountered, one in particular is indelible in my memory: the physical assault by a white boy when I was 13 years old. At the time, I was a new (and the only) Asian student at Globe Junior High School, in Globe, Arizona (a rural town of approximately 20,000 people). For weeks, a decent-looking white boy would stare at me as I made my way to school each morning. I mistakenly thought that his stare was a sign of his admiration, if not a genuine curiosity of another race. But on the school bus one morning, he tapped me on the shoulder. When I turned my head to face him, he suddenly grabbed my hair with the full force of his left hand and, with his right index finger pointing at my nose, hollered: "Why don't you go back to your yellow country!" I thought I was in some kind of trance since the statement, which in reality only lasted for a couple of seconds, kept playing in my mind like a bad dream. I remember hearing the loud shrieking laughs of my peers ringing inside my head, while the driver, who paid no attention to what was happening, drove on. No one on the bus even budged to help me. It seemed that, for them, this was a form of entertainment, and it felt as if they wished to make it last as long as possible. To me, it seemed as if they were an enthused audience that was clapping, laughing, and stamping their feet, all of which made it seem to me as if they were sanctioning the humiliation of the new Asian girl. Worse yet, for the rest of the school year, the bus ride to school made me feel anxious. I kept reliving the awful experience over and over again in my head. In fact, the constant anxiety I felt made me incapable of putting myself in open areas on campus. It impaired me to the extent that I felt I was in a warzone. This war was about "them" versus "me," an Asian immigrant who looked nothing like them.

Needless to say, I was a lonely 8th grader who hated recess and lunch period with every fiber in my being. I never knew what to do or where to hide during those hours. During recess hours, while most of the kids crowded in locker halls lively multitasking—grooming, exchanging love notes, and cracking jokes—I performed one single task in the girl's bathroom. I observed my watch behind the stall door. I sat there for the entire recess period, intently counting down to the last couple of minutes before the bell so I could get to my next class early enough to minimize attention. During the longer lunch periods, I was a bit more adventurous. I snuck out of the school building and hid my body behind the trunk of a huge shady tree. I never dared to sit on its ground in fear of looking idle and lonely to a few occasional passersby (usually students and teachers). So for the entire lunch period, I "attached" my body to this tree by leaning against it as tightly as I could hoping to camouflage myself. Every day, I faithfully and covertly carried out this secretive mission. In my mind, playing the part of this invisible Asian girl was the best option because my other option would have been too cruel to relive—the rude awakening to my otherness, followed by rejection or even assaults by the xenophobes at school.

During that entire miserable school year, this episode on the bus—the aggression of one white boy against one Korean immigrant girl of sensitive age and the tacit approval of thirty-some onlookers (students and one adult driver)—was never reported to the school authorities. In my mind, I felt that the boy knew, and I knew, that anything I said would be futile against him in the principal's office. Although this was not the only situation that forced me to face the *otherness* in me, it was one of the worst, and is a reflection of the racial hatred and division that still exists in the United States.

Since then, I have come to detest the fact that my limited English at that time prevented me from objecting to the cruelty and animosity that I faced. In fact, I hated being limited by my second language ability since my rudimentary English only allowed me to produce what I felt was unsophisticated murmurings to defend myself from my teenage native English-speaking peers. In my mind, I was left with two options: One, succumb to what seemed to be a larger-than-life white boy, who, to me at the time, represented the whole United States, or, two, master the English language, so that I would be equipped to fight back. I chose the second option. Thus, this white boy on that traumatic morning unwittingly ignited in me a passion to excel in English, that I, as a young child, perceived to be the language of the elites.

I became a devoted student of English. By the time I went to college, I was proficient in English. I focused on becoming an articulate speaker so that, whether in academic discussions or in social interactions, I would be able to express my views and opinions freely, with purpose and sophistication. I have been able to achieve this goal. At times, the force of my arguments, combined with my liberal demeanor, has shocked my peers and professors and successfully dispelled many of the stereotypical images of Asian women as passive, silent, and obedient. On campus, I became known as the Asian girl who spoke her mind without fear. Indirectly, this was a way for me to let the boy from Arizona know that, ultimately, he had failed to strip me of my pride in being Korean, and most of all, of my human dignity.

With my proficiency in English, however, new and unanticipated dilemmas in terms of my identity began to surface. My endeavor to master English, which initially started as a means to protect my Koreanness, lost its original shape and purpose. Slowly and inevitably my American education transformed me into an "almost American," leaving few traces of my Korean cultural values. It was only when I went to live in Taiwan for six years that, to my surprise, I discovered I was neither singularly American nor Korean. In Taipei, I was happy to have met some Koreans, but because they were more conservative than the Korean-Americans who I had associated with in the United States, they did not accept me socially as one of their own. In fact, I was sometimes ostracized for being too American. They did not appreciate my outspokenness, an attribute that I had deliberately and strategically cultivated in the United States, ironically, to defend my Korean pride and dignity. Thus although I maintained a professional relationship with the Koreans I worked with, socially, I was drawn more toward, and learned to love, the more egalitarian language and culture of Chinese people.

The Chinese were more accepting of my assertiveness and American sociability, seeing it as a cosmopolitan trait. Unlike the more geopolitically and linguistically homogeneous Koreans, the Chinese were more heterogeneous due to their multiple geopolitical origins and dialects. Their language and mannerisms have evolved to become more cosmopolitan and egalitarian, as opposed to the Koreans, whose honorific system of language and etiquette is still intact after thousands of years. For instance, to this day, Koreans, not only speak but act out their honorifics—for example, by bowing their heads ninety degrees to show their respect to elders when they say *hello.* Most of the honorifics in the Chinese language, however, fell out of use initially at the end of Imperial China but more completely after the Cultural Revolution. The Chinese thus hardly ever bow their heads to say *hello* to their elders. What all this meant was that the more culturally progressive Chinese—contrary to Koreans—were less prone to be offended by strong, opinionated women like me and I, in turn, loved them back because of their tolerance.

I soon started to feel more Chinese than Korean, while maintaining my Americanness. What has evolved from these sometimes painful, but ultimately illuminating cross-cultural experiences, is that I am now very uncomfortable with a single, closely fitting mantle of national identity (i.e., "Korean"). In fact, instead, of the exclusive and distinctive term "Korean American," I now claim an even more inclusive identity as, "Asian American."

Sometimes I feel that even this new title Asian American, is too restricting, especially in light of the fact that I am an Angelino [a resident of Los Angeles, California] who socializes with peoples of all cultures. As Cohen (1997) hypothesizes, as a member of a postmodern cultural diaspora, I ultimately and inevitably have dubious political allegiances. That is, although I maintain certain sociopolitical ties with my legal country (the United States), my motherland (Korea), and the host countries of Taiwan and China, because I do not completely assimilate to any of these national/cultural norms, I live in what Cohen (1997) calls "no-group lands" (p. 189). In this no-group land, my identity is transient and culturally fluid. In tiny increments, I have gradually come to embrace myself as what Bhabha (1998) calls a "postcolonial cultural freak" (pp. 1331–1344)—an indistinguishable, marginalized, and multicultural member of society. Now, I accept and even thrive on the fact that my identity cannot be fixed to one national/cultural locale. It is in constant flux; I simultaneously feel that I am Korean, Chinese, and North American, and lately, an Angelino. Tomorrow, perhaps, I will consider myself a denizen of the entire world.

Although I am at peace with fluidity, others have, at times, tried to give it a definite shape and have attempted to place me into categories. My first advisor in the English department of the college that I was attending was among this group. I told her that I wanted to major in English but also that eventually I was interested in pursuing a graduate degree in TESOL because I always had a dream of becoming an ESL teacher. She told me that if teaching ESL was my goal, I didn't need to major in English, that I could major in TESL (an undergraduate program offered). When I insisted on majoring in English first, she doubtfully questioned: "Are you sure that you really want to do this? Why would you want to put yourself through something that requires much more work?" I did not understand why she was recommending TESL instead of English as an undergraduate degree. Why was she so concerned that I would not survive as an English major? I wondered if it was because there were very few Asian students in the English department. I wondered if it was because she might think that to be an English major one needed to be a native speaker of English. These are questions to which I will never have the answers.

Ironically, by the time I had proven my aptitude as an independent thinker and writer in English (graduating cum laude) and was ready to move on to my master's in TESOL, some of my English professors tried to persuade me into staying with their department for a master's in English literature. One Korean-American English professor told me that he had never considered teaching ESL because he knew that he would not enjoy the unrewarding, mundane drills of teaching rudimentary English. He was genuinely concerned that I might not enjoy my future job as an ESL teacher. Another professor, whom I respected greatly, expressed some reservations as well. One day, as she was handing me a recommendation letter, she said: "In my 15 years of teaching, I have said this to only a handful of my students. . . . Jessie, you should pursue a higher degree in literature." What she seemed to be implying was that, in her opinion, TESOL ranks lower than English literature, academically. I thanked her for thinking so highly of me, and left her office. Regardless of what anyone said, my determination to become an ESL teacher could not be shaken.

In such a way, I got to where I am today, a graduate student of TESOL working on a master's thesis. Unlike the English literature professors I know who have distanced themselves from ESL, I want to meet ESL students at the grass-roots level. I believe that the fact that I was once an ESL student will make me a better critic/self-critic of the instructional methodologies I select and implement in the classroom. I believe that my cultural fluidity and sensibility toward ESL students will facilitate a connection with them because I once faced many of the same challenges of being voiceless and feeling marginalized. I want to help them acquire English so that they will be able to protect themselves against future dehumanizing social injustices. I want to teach them English so that they might have the opportunity for political liberation, economic enrichment, and intellectual realization (not that speaking English guarantees any of these). These are the reasons why I chose TESOL. As a member of a transnational diaspora, I am neither an assimilator nor a separatist but like to think of myself as abridging diverse cultures. If teaching ESL inherently entails multiculturalism, then, I believe that I am in the right discipline, for I am a cultural amalgam.

The Cultural Niche of a NNEST

My journey from ESL student to an English and TESOL major shows that, in addition to some of the more recognized advantages of NNESTs—such as their ability to comprehend non-standard accents, teach grammar, and be role models to their students—they offer many sociopolitical benefits. First, I believe they are likely to want to create an empowering classroom for the often marginalized ESL students, since they themselves may have been marginalized. Second, I would argue that because they know firsthand both the difficulties and benefits of being proficient in more than one language, they may actively support, bilingual/dual-language programs and oppose "English-only" policies (policies that are often institutionally enforced through political intimidations, such as standardized exams administered in English only). Third, I also believe that because they have been exposed to more than one language and culture, they are likely to respect, and even expect, what Foucault (1984) calls "heterotopia" (legitimatization of differences) in a classroom, as opposed to "utopia" (upholding one universal view). Fourth, because they are likely to be accustomed to sociopolitical and linguistic adaptations and changes, they may be willing to try innovative materials and methodologies (an idea supported by Amin, 2004).

Taking a wider view, the sociopolitical and cultural flexibility of many NNESTs may equip them to take on more global roles that can help balance the sociopolitical tensions that exist in education. For example, because they understand firsthand the intricacies of simultaneously maintaining loyalties to both their L1 and L2 cultural customs (Bhabha, 1998; Cohen, 1997; Kristeva, 1991), they are more likely to promote the peaceful classroom or departmental coexistence of students or faculty who may have conflicting cultural, national, political, and/or religious allegiances (e.g., Mexicans vs. Mexican-Americans or Christians vs. Muslims). Thus, because many NNESTs have personally experienced the sometimes harsh reality of conflicts between their first and second cultures (e.g., Arab Americans torn by the political turmoil between their home countries and the United States), they are likely to be adept in negotiating, mitigating, and/or contesting situations or assumptions that threaten heterogeneity in the classroom, skills that are invaluable in a leader. Therefore, considering the numerous implications of their multicultural subjectivity, NNESTs are in a key position to facilitate fair and balanced power dynamics in educational settings.

I believe that a NNEST who has gone through the process of learning a second/third language can evolve to become what I call an ambassador of transnationalism and interculturalism: *transnationalism* in the sense that the NNEST's presence in the classroom helps loosen national borders or extreme nationalism, and *interculturalism* in the sense that the NNEST is the very product of intercultural exposures and intercultural learning of at least two or more cultures (McKay, 2002; Velasco-Martin, 2004). In my case, multicultural influences from Korea, the United States, and Taiwan reduced my singular nationalism and gave me a blend of interculturalism that identifies me. Other NNESTs will have different cultural influences, and all of them are not only legitimate (Canagarajah, 1999, 2005; Widdowson, 1994) but will also become equalizing and harmonizing agents both in the classroom and in the educational system as a whole.

Reflection Question

An underlying theme in this chapter is the idea that issues of race and language are intertwined. To what extent is it the language teacher's responsibility to integrate curriculum that addresses these issues in the classroom?

CHAPTER 3

Narrating One's Life: Autobiographies Problematizing the Notion of "Inner Circle Legitimacy"

Have there ever been instances in which you felt like "the other"? And how did you react to this? Did you try to fit in or distance yourself?

This chapter presents autobiographies by Jeremy C. Kelley, Valerie J. Callet and Shannon Ladymon. These teachers are white and were born in the United States. One might assume that their journeys to become ESL/EFL teachers was unproblematic, but that would be wrong. As they explain in their autobiographies, these teachers, much like those in the previous chapter, were perceived as outsiders, in some cases by themselves and in others by others. These autobiographies show that being white does not necessarily mean that one is a speaker of standard English (Jeremy C. Kelley's case), that one is perceived to be a "legitimate" teacher (Valerie J. Callet), or that one can easily fit into a linguistic community (Shannon Ladymon).

From English to Englishes: A Native English Speaker's Language Learning Journey

JEREMY C. KELLEY
University of California, Los Angeles

People are often surprised to find out that I view myself as a second language learner of standard American English (SAE), even though I was born and raised in Alabama and consider myself to be a native speaker of American English. This statement might be a little difficult to comprehend for some, especially since the majority of the world tends to view American English as a singular, cohesive variety; however, my linguistic and cultural explorations tell me otherwise.

Through reflective analysis of my own personal experiences, I explore the concept of being a non-standard native speaker of English and what that has meant for me as a language teaching professional. Drawing on various aspects of my identity, I demonstrate how these experiences have influenced my teaching of second language pronunciation and how they have in turn led to the development and application of a range of activities designed to expand our awareness of linguistic diversity, all the while calling into question the myth of the elusive goal of native speaker articulatory proficiency.

From English to "Englishes"

Growing up in the rural South, I sounded just like everyone else around me. I had no concept of the distinct features that differentiated my English from that of the many other "Englishes" (Jenkins, 2006, p. 157) of both the United States and of the rest of the world. The neighbor called the thing that you push around the grocery store a *buggy*, just like me, and the principal at my high school would always make suggestions by saying things such as *Y'all might should…*, to which I would most certainly reply with a prompt, *Yes, sir, I'm fixin' to.* I was comfortable with who I was and in the identity that I had developed as a native English speaker. In fact, I never knew that this way of speaking, this variety of English that I spoke, was in any way out of the ordinary because it was quite simply the only variety that I had ever known. I was certainly aware that southerners had an accent, also known as the southern drawl, but I had no idea that the language was, in so many respects, so distinct from other English varieties that it would one day come to be both a problematic marker of my differentness and a sense of pride in my life. My way of speaking was, for lack of a better term, normative, in that both I and those around me shared a linguistic intersubjectivity that reified and reproduced a local sense of belonging, manifest through a common experience of cultural and linguistic expressivity. In Eckert and McConnel-Ginet's (1992) terms, we were a community of practice in which speaking southern was the norm, with all of our resulting linguistic practices representing a reflection of our common sense of shared identity.

The moment I left Alabama and went to begin my new life in New York City as a cost engineer in the fashion industry, I realized how much my identity as a person was interconnected with my language identity. The northeastern United States, for a small-town country boy like me, was culture shock to say the least. The pace was fast, and the people slowed down for no one. To me, at least in the beginning, New York was a cold, lonely place. All I had was myself and my new job, and both of those elements were about to be culturally and linguistically tested.

Upon arriving in New York, the few coworkers that I had had the pleasure of meeting in advance of my relocation had organized an informal dinner with drinks to follow. The dinner went well, with everyone getting along as if we had known each other for years. However, while having drinks at a bar afterward, I experienced my first taste of what it meant to truly be an outsider, and it all came down to the language that I spoke.

While at the bar, our group had begun speaking with an adjacent group, upon which I entered into direct one-on-one conversation with one of our new acquaintances. Immediately after introducing myself, my southern identity became apparent through my accented speech. The person with whom I was speaking instantly noted my accent and proceeded to inquire where exactly I was from. After explaining my origins, he then proceeded to explain to me how New York, and by extension the New Yorkers that inhabit it, are filled with culture. To support his claim, he referenced the museums, the ballet, the opera, the theater, the array of ethnic cuisine, and of course the multicultural population. With all of these aspects I agreed, as New York is indeed known to be a cultural melting pot with events, attractions, and people from all corners of the globe at every turn. However, his next statement gave me reason to pause and reflect on my preliminary agreements. Without really knowing anything about me, he proceeded to inform me that southerners "just don't have any real culture, at least not any that rivals New York's culture," all the while smiling as if nothing offensive had left his lips. My response, I must admit, was not kind. The first thing that I managed to articulate, after gathering my thoughts, was that museums were nothing more than a collection of other people's cultures, and that being multicultural meant existing within a conglomeration of various other world cultures, which does not translate into a cohesive indigenous culture unto itself. My point was that, of the various aspects that he had mentioned, there was no underlying feature that marked them as distinctly belonging to New York, other than their location. Needless to say, our first impressions of each other were not good. Indeed, within minutes our conversation had dwindled into nothingness, with each of us gently removing ourselves from the one-on-one interaction into the safety of our own groups.

What struck me about this interaction was that our asymmetrical perspectives on culture seemed to have been derived exclusively from my being marked as a speaker of Southern American English. My accent had seemingly indexed an intrinsic facet of my identity, and that felt to me as if it was used by my interlocutor in a way that inadvertently managed to subordinate my native English speaker identity as inferior to that of those around me. That night I realized just how different my identity as a native speaker was from other native speaker identities, and that realization was not comforting, especially given that I was made to feel inferior within moments of arriving at my new city of residence.

My first professional struggle with language identity in New York came a few weeks later when I had to give a presentation in front of a panel of my superiors. Thinking that I did not miss a beat in carrying out my task with flawless precision, I felt as though I had pulled off a major accomplishment in my new career. However, as I was wrapping things up and opening the floor for questions, I was jolted back into reality by a coworker who found it necessary to stand up, politely say, *Excuse me,* and then tell me, in one of the strongest New York accents that I have ever heard, that she did not understand a single word that I had just said, and that it would be most appreciated if I would run through it all again, more slowly and "clearer." At that moment, as I shockingly began to prepare myself for another go at the presentation, I knew that my language identity, that of the young, comfortable professional trying out something new in a new place, had just received the rudest awakening imaginable. In an instant I had been publicly marked as a cultural, as well as a linguistic, outsider, even though I was still in my country of birth, and thus in a place where I had assumed that my identity would be viewed as the same. This represented a crucial factor in the development of my language identity because, as Kubota and Lin (2009) state, "Whiteness exerts its power as an invisible and unmarked norm against which all Others are racially and culturally defined, marked, and made inferior" (p.10); and yet, it was not my *whiteness* that had set me apart and marked me as different from my new environment, but my language, even though my native dialect was representative of "the largest dialect area in the United States" (MacNeil & Cran, 2005, p. 67). In fact, "more Americans now 'speak Southern' than speak any other regional dialect" (MacNeil & Cran, 2005, p. 67). After reflecting on what this meant, and recomposing myself, I quickly realized that I had lost the comfort of in-group status, of my sense of identity that I had shared with my southern community of practice, and I was now teetering on the edge of a linguistically alien frontier that did not recognize my linguistic identity as valid, relegating it instead to the position of an *inferior majority* given the fact that it represented the largest American English dialect, only outside of its traditional borders.

What was perplexing to me, especially in regard to both of the aforementioned incidences, was that my variety of English was not always seen as problematic. Indeed, casual conversational encounters in shops and parks often had much more positive outcomes. Most people seemed delighted upon hearing my accent, telling me that it was "cute" or "friendly." The only difference that I could discern from the various encounters and experiences was that in each negative case there was often a power variable, or at least a perceived power variable. In the bar conversation, the person with whom I spoke was, in essence, showing off. Prior to our cultural disagreement, he had been boasting about his job in what seemed to be a bid for attention from anyone who might oblige. His self-centered approach to the interaction implied that he envisioned himself as more important than others, and I believe to this day that any change in focus that removed him from the spotlight would have been interpreted as a threat to his perceived position of power (as object of the conversation). As a result, in a single statement, misguided and ignorantly derived though it may have been, he was able to undermine my position, which had become the object of focus within the interaction, through the perpetuation of stereotypes associated with my linguistic variety. For those not familiar with the stereotypes associated with Southern American English, I mean words like *backwoods, hillbilly, farmer, peasant,* all of which imply a sense of being uneducated, unsophisticated, uncultured. Thus through the activation of a schematic field of associative identities, he was able to systematically relegate my identity to a subordinate position within the interaction, shifting the balance of perceived power back into his hands. In the workplace example, power also played a role. However, in this example, it was not a perceived power differential but an overt one resulting from asymmetries in the corporate chain of command. In denigrating my presentation, my coworker, who was in fact my superior, was able to simultaneously assert her own position of power while marking my position as subservient. When viewed together these examples illustrate how interactants are consciously processing phonological linguistic features and exercising power in response to said features as a means of reifying their own social standing, even when it is at the cost of the social standing of others.

It was after these events, and upon definitively realizing my status as *other,* that I made a conscious decision to learn a new language, one that would give me new in-group status and comfort in my adopted surroundings. It was then that I decided to make SAE my second language because, as Peirce (1995) points out, "If learners invest in a second language, they do so with the understanding that they will acquire a wider range of symbolic and material resources, which will in turn increase the value of their cultural capital" (p. 17), with cultural capital here representing "the knowledge and modes of thought that characterize different classes and groups in relation to specific sets of social forms" (Bourdieu, as cited in Peirce, 1995, p. 17).

The next actions that I took came to define the person that I wanted to become. Although it was difficult at first, I began by addressing the issue of my *differentness*. I made it my priority to blend in with the locals, which ultimately meant that my aim was to be as comprehensible as I could possibly be, eliminating the spoken markers that challenged my candidacy as a viable member of the local community of practice in New York. In-group status became my primary objective. I no longer wanted to be seen as *other*, because *other*, here synonymous with *different*, was problematic. I was embarking on what Liu (2004) calls a journey of "adaptive cultural transformation" (p. 28). I would no longer permit myself to be excluded from or subordinated within local society; rather, I would adopt local society's version of normativity into my identity, allowing it to hybridize with old traits in order to create something new, something that would grant me both cultural and linguistic access to my new surroundings.

I began training myself as if my life depended on it, and to some degree, given my work situation, it did. The variety of English spoken in the New York area became the "prestige" (Meyerhoff, 2006, p. 37) goal, as I diligently began working on my pronunciation at home, making a conscious effort to adapt to my new linguistic environment. I also found friends with whom I could safely practice and experiment with new forms and registers of the language. Over time, I no longer viewed it as simply learning the target language, rather I saw it as an investment. As Peirce (1995) demonstrates, "Investment in the target language is . . . an investment in a learner's own social identity, an identity which is constantly changing across time and space" (p. 18). In time, the more prominent features of my southern dialect drastically reduced (which says a lot about how strong it must have been considering that I speak with relatively strong southern features still today), and I learned how to suppress the double modals, the *ma'ams* and *sirs*, and the unknown lexical items that perplexed my northern interlocutors. Nevertheless, I was incapable of eliminating all of the prominent features like the second-person plural pronoun *y'all,* which marks my speech as much today as it did in my early childhood. In time I almost completely blended in with my new environment, becoming what Hansen (2004) would call an "invisible minority" (p. 40) given the fact that I looked like the idealized version of an American English speaker (i.e., white), but when I opened my mouth to speak, certain intrinsic characteristics that marked me as different persisted.

As my speech transformed, things began to improve, both socially and professionally. It seemed as though I had successfully transformed my Southern American English identity, which did not seem to fit in very well in other parts of the country, into a new identity that embraced the local lingo and more comfortably blended in. I felt less and less like an outsider in my new environment and more like an in-group member, although the same could not be said for my status back home in Alabama.

We claim that "one dialect is as good as another, [but] in reality we have not practiced what we have preached" (Newmeyer, 1973, p. 47). Over time, my identity as a southerner became more and more marginal; this was an ongoing shift that continues to some degree even today. My close family bonds became more distant and strained as I sounded and carried myself in a culturally and linguistically non-southern manner. In fact, to my family back home, I had become an outsider because my linguistic identity had evolved so extensively that is was foreign to their ears. In retrospect, I see that I had unwittingly placed myself into a sort of linguistic limbo that was no longer southern, and yet not quite northern either.

Soon I realized that, in adding SAE to my linguistic repertoire, I was giving up elements that had defined my existence since birth. In short, I was exchanging parts of my original identity for something that was seen by the world around me as more desirable, all for the sake of being culturally accepted and not being viewed as a marked other in my own country. In doing so, I exemplified the way in which we, both speakers of non-standard forms of English and nonnative speakers of English, have dealt linguistic power to "a minority of people who have the power to impose it" (Widdowson, 1994, p. 379). This is an important point in that "limiting learners' exposure to only one or two of the infinite variations of L1 and L2 varieties and representing them as universal norms denies the realities of the repertoires of World Englishes learners encounter when they go out into the real world" (Burns, 2005, pp. 5–6).

Yet the harsh, ever-present reality of linguistic hegemony is that it must reify itself in relation to subordinate varieties, which challenge its authority (Briggs, 1998). And this notion of hegemony was, as I was coming to understand, the root of my transformation in identity. I was beginning to understand the sociopolitical implications of something as "simple" as accent and how it could have such heavily weighted implications on everyday life events. More importantly, I was coming to realize that the features that I had grown up with were a part of me, and a part of my identity as a native speaker of English. In more concise words, I was beginning to see that we are not all the same, and that a world limited to a single voice, a single language, loses much.

Becoming a Lover of Languages

Despite my growing awareness that my identity was in a continuous state of progression, in time I noticed that New Yorkers began to understand virtually everything that I said and that the number of repeats that I would have normally been obliged to perform in conversational exchanges was dwindling. My *differentness* was becoming but a minuscule hint in the underlying issue of my linguistic identity. Of course my accent was still there, but it had become, in my opinion, charming rather than troublesome. The foreign nature of my southern speech characteristics began to represent a secondary rather than a primary facet of who I was as a person. My identity had changed, linguistically evolving in order to more comprehensively accommodate the new language milieu to which I had been striving to belong.

Over the next four years, I continued my seizure and solidification of in-group status, eventually shedding most of the marginality that had plagued my earlier days in New York. I excelled professionally, being promoted to upper management, and had a social life that I would not have traded for anything. However, another major life shift was waiting around the corner. In undergoing the process of becoming a speaker of SAE, I realized that my passion for languages ran deeper than I ever thought it would. Given this, after careful consideration and self-reflection, I decided that I wanted to study a foreign language, and I began directing all of my attention toward French.

Studying day and night, I began by coaching myself with tapes and small glosses of the most frequently used words and phrases, and soon I had fallen head over heels in love with my third language. I was so in love that I decided to return to college in order to work with French full time. I also dabbled in other languages, developing both a substantial awareness of the internal mechanics of Spanish and a superficial understanding of Dutch, but French, the language that I had grown to adore, remained my passion. Eventually I would attain a level of proficiency that would deceive both other learners, as well as the ears of native speakers.

Once, while at the University of California, Los Angeles, the university that I had later attended for my language studies, a native speaker of French, who had shared many classes with me, was shocked to find out that I was not a native speaker as well. She said that she knew that I was not from France, but she always thought that French had been my first language. This was, in my opinion at the time, one of the highest compliments that an adult language learner could possibly receive from a native speaker of a language. However, the very notion that I sounded like a native French speaker was confusing, at best, because as I had come to reevaluate the meaning of my status as a native speaker of English, I had also come to reevaluate the very broad concept of what it is to be and sound like a native speaker in general. In looking back, I believe that the reason that my classmate mistook me for a native French speaker was because of the importance of the non-standard English language characteristics that had defined my identity up to and upon leaving Alabama and venturing into a linguistically unfamiliar region of the English-speaking world. Throughout my journey, my focus had been so heavily centered on proper pronunciation in SAE that I transferred this mentality over to my learning of French. This might seem strange considering that I was learning French in the United States without any environmental pressures to perform like a native speaker, but pronunciation had become my primary focus, and ultimately my greatest linguistic achievement. My original language identity insecurities had somehow led me to subconsciously strive for the most refined French pronunciation that I could possibly achieve. In short, my struggle to sound normal in SAE had in fact transferred over to my subsequent language learning endeavors, perpetuating the idea that the dominant variety's societal construction (in this case Parisian French) is the one to which all learners should strive, which in turn heavily influences both the mind of the language learner, and of the language instructor (Jenkins, 2005). Discovering this for myself, I concluded that my "remodeled" language identity was in serious need of new direction and of new perspectives. The linguistic domination of my heritage language had compromised my very being, and this, to me, was unacceptable. I was, for the second time, realizing that my southernness, and the linguistic variation that accompanied it, was something to be celebrated rather than hidden, particularly given the rich nature of its phonological, syntactic, and lexical contributions to the English language. In fact, after contemplating the status of my southern dialect, I became enraged at the notion that a speaker of a non-standard variety could be relegated to an inferior linguistic status by those that use the prestige, or "correct" dialect, just because political and economic advantages have allowed them to perpetuate the idea of their superiority at the expense of others. Given this growing belief in the validity of my linguistic origins, I decided that the best way that I could challenge and counter the hegemonic nature of the standard variety was to become a language teacher myself. To accomplish this I did two things: I enrolled in a graduate program in TESOL and I took a job as a teacher of ESL.

Back to English, and on to the Classroom

After gaining the experience of an English language teaching professional and working diligently to challenge the hidden assumptions of standard variety English, I have finally found comfort in my language identity. I no longer view my southernness as a handicap but as something to be proud of and embraced. I have discovered that, although the form of English that I grew up with and that influences my speech even today is different from the many other "Englishes" (Jenkins, 2006, p. 157) of the world, it has validity all the same, especially given the fact that it is now the most prolific American variety (MacNeil & Cran, 2005). I no longer try to hide my heritage language for fear of seeming unintelligent or "country"; instead, I wear it as a badge of honor, returning it to its rightful place in my personal and linguistic identities.

As a teacher of ESL speech and pronunciation, the experiences of my own language learning journey greatly impact my teaching. My phonological and lexical ups and downs in learning SAE have triggered an awareness that constantly shines through in my ESL classroom. I draw on my personal struggles in language assimilation to demonstrate the range of variety found within English, and the fact that, although there are many forms, no single form should reign supreme or have precedence over the others. For me, it is important that my students understand that "the majority of those who are to the language born speak non-standard English and have themselves to be instructed in the standard at school" (Widdowson, 1994, p. 379), which is, in fact, exactly the case in my own English language learning experience. Relying on this real-life evidence, I try to help my students understand that there are many English varieties and extend that knowledge to teach them that the words *accent* and *dialect* do not equal *deficiency*. I want them to see themselves, and the teachers that instruct them, as individuals with linguistic potential and individuality, regardless of societal, political, linguistic, or racial issues that might dictate otherwise.

As stated by Medgyes (2001), "All outstanding teachers are ideal in their own way, and as such are different from each other" (p. 440). Therefore, to help my students develop a sense of appreciation for differences in accents and dialects, I employ a range of activities that, although not always traditional, are readily accessible to students in the United States and are quickly becoming accessible in EFL settings as well. One such activity is to bring in either actual English speakers (which might be more difficult for EFL communities) or recordings of English speakers (a resource that is becoming increasingly accessible given the extensive reach of films and the internet) that come from a variety of places.

I have introduced a multitude of accents this way; most are well received with little apprehension, but others often lead to rather interesting discussions as to what it means to be a native speaker of English. For example, when I played a recording of a Jamaican English speaker, students' expressions immediately changed. One student even went so far as to ask for different materials that would showcase "real" English, rather than, as he put it, "people who are learning the language." This led to a content-based educational discussion on the country of Jamaica and its history as an English-speaking nation. Some students were surprised that I would group this variety of English with the more commonly known forms of SAE and British Received Pronunciation (RP); however, as I explained the diverse nature of English and its position as a language of the world they slowly began to accept the Jamaican variety as a valid form, which both shares with and differs from other varieties in phonological and syntactic features.

Expanding Circle communities can also adopt this type of linguistic analysis. Although it is important to realize that Expanding Circle settings might contain only one home language, class discussions and activities can focus on local dialects and non-standard varieties of the home language as a means to linguistic awareness and, ultimately, as a means of propagating linguistic acceptance. By incorporating the notion of linguistic diversity into the language program and showing variation in home country varieties, a good example for English varieties can also be set. Thus, by identifying the value of local variation, students can begin to appreciate target language variation.

Another activity that I have found to increase students' awareness of English variation is role-playing. However, rather than having them adhere to SAE, I introduce a range of English varieties that represent Inner, Outer, and Expanding Circle varieties (Kachru, 1996). Some might consider this activity to be a perpetuation of stereotypes through imitation that could easily be misconstrued as sarcastic mimicry; however, the focus of the activity is not on the various racial/ethnic, class, or cultural distinctions that often accompany linguistic varieties, but to showcase subtle nuances within and between varieties that mark them as different, and thus as potential recipients of subordinate positioning in relation to dominant forms. After showcasing what the accent in question might sound like, either by replicating it myself or by bringing in recordings or clips of films, the students are given a script that they will practice. I typically prefer to limit this activity to one accent every two weeks to familiarize them with the many variants without creating confusion, especially given the fact that I am mandated to teach "American" English. The students then, in pairs, attempt to recreate the variety to the best of their abilities, based on the in-class presentation of forms or on the supplemental video/audio recordings used to model the variety in question. As some of these sounds are new to them, they might briefly falter in performing the task, but the benefits are that they have a good time and they are exposed to English variation. After they have practiced for a while, volunteers are invited to perform their dialogue for the whole class, which often leads to a thought-provoking concluding discussion about whether the variety in question is in fact a valid form of English.

An example of this activity would be, on one day, using RP English (i.e., the Queen's English) and on another day using Cockney English (a non-standard variety frequently spoken alongside RP in the United Kingdom). Students quite often have difficulties in reproducing these forms but come away from the activity with a new awareness of linguistic diversity that helps them to see the immense amount of variation present within English as it is spoken across the globe. To ensure that these role-playing activities are not misconstrued as a perpetuation of stereotypes, I often provide students with a content-based extension of the activity through historical facts. For example, I show them statistical information on the British Isles, which illustrates how RP is in reality a minority among British English dialects, all the while maintaining its status as an international prestige. I also provide examples of the lyrical uniqueness of Cockney English, which marks it as an acoustic-centered variety of English through its rich usage of rhyme and slang. The goal is that students begin to see value in what has been historically classified as unimportant (i.e., Cockney), and learn to question the enforced value of historically promoted varieties (i.e., RP), all the while expanding their knowledge of, and thus ability to, utilize language as a tool for navigating the sociopolitical hurdles that accompany diverse articulatory expression.

Another activity that I like to incorporate, although it represents the most basic of teaching activities, is to use explicit instruction of language variation. Some students seem to thrive on this type of instruction that, in my perspective, receives less credit than it is due. For example, after illustrating the fact that native English-speaking Californians, pronounce the word *caught* as [kat] —which to the Eastern United States would signify a *cot,* or a portable bed that guests might sleep in, rather than the past tense of the verb *to catch*—students were quick to reintroduce this fact in subsequent lessons, particularly when this phonological representation was involved. I have even heard side discussions in which one student informed another that "in California it is said this way, but in the East it is said that way." This example suggests that explicit instruction can promote linguistic awareness, which, in turn, may result in a recognition of the validity of regional variation.

A final activity that helps my students appreciate the diversity of the English language is various forms of ethnographic research. One form is to have the students watch reality television programs in which they hear people from all over the United States and often from all over the world. I ask them to record some of the interesting variation that they encounter, and later we discuss it in class. However, since most of my students are new to the United States and are not familiar with American television programs, I frequently use a backup form of ethnographic research in which students go out into the community and examine the English that they hear around them, be it spoken by native speakers or nonnative speakers. Although this might be more difficult in an EFL setting, teachers could have students visit tourist areas that are frequently visited by English-speaking travelers. As in the ESL setting, this could be of great value to EFL learners because it allows them to hear the language in authentic usage, and to see just how non-standard, shortened, and ungrammatical everyday speech can be, particularly among native speakers.

Strangely enough, I am frequently drawn to a question posed by Liu (2004) in relation to NNESTs, "How can we as nonnative speakers of English take advantage of our experience learning the language" (p. 37)? As a person who sees himself as a native speaker of English, this might seem like a curious selection from which to cite, but as someone who spoke a form of English that was always seen as inferior to the dominant varieties, I can relate to the feeling of nonnativeness. Although I would never want to belittle the experiences of the nonnative speaker of English, my personal struggles form a unique, and yet interestingly parallel example that sheds new insight on the idea of "World Englishes" (Jenkins, 2006, p.157).

To conclude, the language-teaching community should avoid occupying itself with the unrealistic goal of attaining "British" or "American" model dialects. Instead, it should begin to examine the issue from a global point of view by examining how each of the many native and nonnative varieties constitute the global context. In striving for a native model, we have to ask ourselves, can this really be attained? The question of the native speaker and of the native speaker variety becomes too complex and difficult to define given the fact that native speakers themselves do not, in most cases, speak the standard prestige variety. What this means for pedagogy is that we must challenge the assumptions of native speaker status in order to develop language teaching philosophies and methodologies that will provide the best possible learning experiences and models for an ever-changing and ever-growing group of language learners and users. Much can be drawn from the native varieties, but the global nature of English as it stands today can no longer be denied. The diverse nature of what it means to be a user of modern English—standard variety native speakers, non-standard variety native speakers, nonnative speakers who have achieved near native proficiency, and those who simply identify with the language in question—leaves us with no choice but to view English as a living entity that adapts to the environment in which it finds itself. No longer limited to the British Isles, North America, and Australia, the English language has become a precious commodity used by millions worldwide, and it is time to acknowledge it as such by showcasing its complexity, rather than restricting it to a linguistic code determined by the speech patterns of one group of users.

Amidst the Fog, I See Clearly for a Moment

VALERIE J. CALLET
University of Southern California

Background

The power of education and of educators can be significant. When I was an undergraduate in the college of education at a large university in Pennsylvania, a speaker was invited to talk to our class, which consisted mostly of white students. She was an African-American principal from a school in Philadelphia. The year was 1995, but I still remember two powerful things she said. The first was about affirmative action. She likened life to a race in which certain people got a head start, and affirmative action was one way to ensure that others who were held back could catch up. Second, she said that when people meet, they first notice sex and then race. Her message, delivered in such a direct but non-accusatory way, stuck with me, and she opened my eyes to critical issues in education that I would face throughout my career.

After graduating in 1996, I worked in several schools including a large urban district in Northern California, which had a reputation for having too many white teachers, considering the student population. At my school, only about 7 percent of our students were white, but the staff was nearly 100 percent white. The director of the school was a white male. It was evident that white people had a head start in the race and were still running. I left the district after only a year.

Fortunately, my current school in Long Beach, California, has a staff that closely mirrors the student population. In this narrative, I will discuss some of the challenges I have faced at this job as a white teacher serving primarily students of color among a staff of color, and how I came to reconcile the fact that, although I am a member of a privileged race, I can still be an effective educator. The story lacks a happy ending, but I believe it is hopeful, nonetheless. Through the cultivation of "relationships based on mutual caring" (Raible & Irizarry, 2007, p. 192) with individuals different from me, I have grown as a teacher and a person.

I continue to worry that by positioning myself as the subject of the narrative, and thus focusing on whiteness, I may be participating in the ideology of white domination (Raible & Irizarry, 2007). Granted, it is my story. At the same time, what would it be without my gentle teachers? My hope is to provide some insights and suggestions for future educators of all races and ethnicities, particularly those working with students who are different than they are.

Literature

In the United States, whites have greater access to employment and educational opportunity; they occupy positions of power and privilege of which they are often unaware (Delpit, 2006a; Gollnick & Chinn, 2002; Johnson, 2002; Sleeter, 2005). Bourdieu (1994), for instance, argued that people in power have greater access to opportunities in society, including education. Along similar lines, Delpit (2006a) noted that middle-class white children are privy to mainstream American culture, including knowledge of standard English, and as such have greater access to the "culture of power" (p. 24). This power culture is apparent in schools, which typically reflect middle-class, European norms (Gay, 2000). Not coincidentally, in educational institutions, white teachers far outnumber teachers of color, and research predicts that this trend will continue (Clark & Flores, 2001; Johnson, 2002; Sleeter, 2005).[1] Peirce (1995) reminds us that power impacts the interactions between "language learners and target language speakers" (p. 12), including the relationships between students and teachers. But do white teachers realize they are granted privileges often withheld from others, including their non-white students? And how, if at all, do they reconcile this power discrepancy to promote equity in the classroom and beyond?

Research on white teacher identity shows that white teachers do not identify themselves in terms of race (Hurtsfield, 1978, as cited in Riojas-Clark & Bustos-Flores, 2001; Mazzei, 1997) but, instead, describe themselves in terms of personal attributes. In an analysis of narratives, white teachers have even been found to be unaware of race, and those who were aware often did not recognize how their whiteness positioned them as privileged members of society (Johnson, 2002).[2] Further, few white teachers have been found to understand the impact of institutionalized racism, and many vehemently deny it exists (Flynn, 2010; Sleeter, 2005). With respect to classroom practices, one study focusing on two teachers (Chubbuck, 2004) revealed some troubling findings. Despite awareness of white privi-

[1]The shortage of minority teachers in the U.S. and ways to increase their representation in the teaching force were the topic of a special issue of *Teacher Education Quarterly* (2007). However, as of 2011, minority teacher representation continued to be a problem. Specifically, a recent report of the U.S. Department of Education (2011) presented statistics showing that the current teaching force in the U.S. does not reflect the diverse student population. According to the report, while 38 percent of the student body is African American or Hispanic, only 14 percent of the teaching force is African American or Hispanic. Additionally, African American or Hispanic male teacher representation is even smaller (2 percent). In order to address this lack of diversity, the U.S. Department of Education (2011) has launched a comprehensive agenda.

[2]Flynn (2010) describes research that supports the idea that white teachers have trouble recognizing the fact that being white makes them "privileged"; to avoid recognizing their own privilege, they often "rely on discourses of colorblindness, meritocracy, and individualism" (p. 167).

lege, both teachers in the study displayed low academic expectations for students of color. While this research is limited in scope, its findings are troubling if we accept the notion that in order to address a problem, we first must admit that there is one and then take responsibility to effect change.

We can find some hope in Johnson's (2002) promising work on white teachers working with ethnic minority students. The teachers in the study built on their other, less-privileged identities to better understand the struggles of their students. Johnson offered several recommendations to increase equity in the classroom, including asking white teachers to experience non-white cultures to gain some insight into their students' struggles. Finally, Mazzei (1997) and Raible and Irizarry (2007) encourage white educators to seek assistance from and build relationships with persons of color to better understand the challenges of their diverse students.[3] I would add that I believe that such relationships can lead to fuller and better lives for all.

Long Beach, California

Without a doubt, the first thing that impressed me about my current school in Long Beach was the interview panel; there was not one white face among them. I thought, *Finally, a staff that represents the student population!* But my first two years on the job were very challenging—and the challenges remain. The problems I face today are similar to those I faced when I was hired. For instance, I find myself eating alone again since Michelle, my colleague and friend, left the school. I have moments when I feel that I have no business working

---

[3]A line of work that has shown promise in promoting teacher awareness about issues of race is the integration of instruction on critical multiculturalism in pre-service teacher preparation. In contrast to liberal multiculturalism, designed to promote what Kubota and Lin (2009) call "a difference-blind egalitarian vision about diverse cultures and peoples" (p. 13), critical multiculturalism is designed to help pre-service teachers (and teachers in general) confront issues of discourse, power, culture, race, and privilege (Flynn, 2010) and, at the same time, learn how integrate critical multiculturalism in their own teaching (e.g., Lea, 2010).

with these students, that I cannot possibly be a role model to them; sadly, one of my newer colleagues recently said this to me despite never observing me teach. In these moments, I think to myself, *I have to get another job; I am no good here, for anyone*. But I have grown as an educator in this setting in ways that I would not have elsewhere.

To back up a bit, in 2000, I was hired as the English teacher at a public, charter high school in Long Beach that serves students ages 16–24 who have dropped out of traditional high schools. At the time, a former graduate of the program, a 20-year-old Latina female named Celia, was teaching the class. The administration had a tradition of hiring former graduates of the program to teach academic courses, but No Child Left Behind (NCLB) was starting to impose a shift in the practice; efforts to seek fully credentialed teachers in all classes had begun. When I took the teaching position, Celia, in effect, was demoted to teacher's assistant. This shift was met by much resistance from the students (60 percent Latino, 30 percent African American), particularly the boys who made up 45 percent of the total student population. I distinctly remember one young man saying, "I wish you would go. You look and act way too much like a teacher." I was obviously an outsider, not just in terms of race (I was the only white person on the staff) but also age (I was 10 years older than Celia). Needless to say, I had difficulty being the teacher of the class, and I am sure Celia had difficulty shifting from teacher to teacher's assistant. I felt society's power structure alive in the class and felt that my whiteness in particular was too conspicuous. I was hyperaware of the culture of power in which I was a member, and I did not want to abuse that power. I felt guilty about being the teacher while Celia became the assistant and, as a result, I believe I was a weak teacher, especially in terms of student discipline.

A big shift occurred when Celia got a new job, and the principal hired Michelle, a middle-aged and highly educated African-American woman. Although Michelle was more educated than I, she was hired as my assistant because her field was not education, and she did not hold a teaching credential. Michelle had served in the Peace Corps like me, and we hit it off right away. She taught me a lot. Whereas Celia had been lenient with the students, Michelle was tough and professional. She was a high-ranking officer in the military and not afraid of the students at all. But she also used humor and sarcasm in the class and she "kept it real"; she spoke truthfully and, when appropriate, told students what they were doing wrong and how to correct their behavior. Moreover, she was not afraid to talk openly about race with me and our students. We were a team, which prevented students from playing us against each other. It is important to note that we did not contradict one another in front of students. Any disagreements were handled after school. We were also friends; the students would see us laughing and going out to lunch together. At the same time, my relationship with the African-American students seemed to be improving markedly. I sensed that they felt more comfortable with me, and fewer African Americans were quitting the class or requesting referrals. Perhaps I picked up the culture and some of the language through Michelle. Perhaps students took a cue from Michelle's acceptance and friendship with me. It is difficult to explain exactly what it was. I was heartbroken when she took a job in another state, but we have remained friends. Michelle taught me that as a teacher, I often have to speak up, but I also have to know when to be direct and when to use humor. She also helped me to stop taking everything and everybody so seriously because mistakes are a part of life, and they can be forgiven.

I also learned some very valuable lessons from the students themselves. I will never forget David, a 17-year-old African American who wrote his persuasive essay on the following topic: "Why White People Are Evil." Initially, I was upset, taking it personally, but he did an excellent job supporting his argument with examples from the past and present, and when I scored his essay on the rubric, he earned an A. Still, I wanted to discuss the paper with him, and I am glad I did. In the course of our discussion, David admitted something to me. He said that he did not really hate white people, but that the opposite is true—that whites hate and fear blacks. I will never forget that conversation. I was ashamed to be white, but at the same time, grateful that he felt comfortable enough to reveal his thoughts to me, a white teacher. To be clear, I am not saying that I do not have difficulties with African-American students anymore. I have trouble with all the students at times, but I am now more aware of their struggles and how I fit into those struggles as a white woman.

A further challenge for me has been learning how to better interact with my Latino students, many of whom speak Spanish. I noticed some of my approaches were not very effective, particularly my sarcasm. Although no one ever said anything to me, I sometimes noticed an embarrassed or hurt look on the faces of some Latino students after I had joked around with them about something they had done. From my current assistant, Carlos, a former graduate of our school who is of Guatemalan descent and a Spanish speaker, I learned that many students became embarrassed if I called attention to their behavior in front of their classmates. Now I watch how Carlos interacts with students, and I mimic his behavior. For instance, regarding discipline, Carlos approaches students quietly to correct their behavior, and he often takes them outside the class to speak with them one-on-one. I have had a lot of success with this approach and not only with my Latino students. In effect, I have had to learn different styles of interaction while constantly adjusting my behavior for individuals.

One persistent source of difficulty, however, is that I cannot speak Spanish. Carlos uses Spanish quite a bit to connect with our Spanish-speaking students, who form the majority of the class. As a result, students feel free to speak Spanish and other home languages as well. It is important to note that Carlos also translates between Spanish and English to include everybody in the conversation. Furthermore, he encourages all of us to learn Spanish through the music that we play in class, which helps to create a learning community that does not stop with the students. Incidentally, one day after school, a few of the Latino students surprised me with a song. I am thankful to work with someone like Carlos who consistently treats all people with dignity and respect. Indeed, he is a role model for all of us.

I have mimicked my peers in an effort to learn how to work better with diverse students in the classroom. I have also made some friends in the process. Here again, it is important to note that my approach often changes with respect to individual students of the same ethnicity. There is no one formula for being an effective teacher. Sometimes I learn too late that the approach I chose was not the right one. I say this because one of our students, Manuel, recently quit school, which left me thinking, "If only I had done something differently. . . ." Despite such heartbreaks, however, I see some progress. Recently, during a teacher's meeting, my boss told the staff that one of our students said she did not like white people. I responded, "I'm not having any difficulty with this student." One of my colleagues laughed and said, "She probably doesn't know you're white." Although I am pretty sure this is not the case, the fact that some of my colleagues can now joke with me about race shows the shift that has taken place in my original outsider status.

Claiming the Right

I am still exploring my role as a white teacher in my current environment. Coupled with my own discomfort about being a member of the dominant culture is the hierarchy in which I work. My school is a unique community in that it is operated by African Americans despite having a student population that is 60 percent Latino. In effect, I have observed the substitution of one hierarchy for another. However, with respect to the larger society, whites are still in power. How then can I create an equitable environment in this classroom that is part of a unique school community, which in turn is part of an even larger society? How can I empower all students and still exercise authority in the classroom? I draw strength and motivation from Peirce's (1995) study of second language students, including Martina, a mother, who "claimed the right to speak" (p. 23). This act allowed her identity as a mother (one who is permitted to speak) to override her identity as an immigrant (one who is forced to be silent). The mother reassigned an identity to herself that would enable her to exercise power in her environment. Similarly, I learned to reassign my identity, as the following example demonstrates.

One student, Jessica, a 19-year-old Mexican American, was not doing her work in class. I told her she was lagging, that she needed to get to work. Jessica laughed and said, "That is exactly what my mom tells me, what you just told me." I claim the right to teach and to care for these young people every day, and this becomes part of my own development. I want them to be successful in school, to feel comfortable and happy in the classroom, and to learn—to have access to the knowledge and language of power—so they can help create a better future. And their successes are my triumphs. In order to reconcile my identity struggle, I replace my identity as a white person with an identity as teacher and caretaker of my students in our classroom.

I have often wished I could be Latina in order to better serve my Latino students. And I have wished to be African American, Filipina, or Samoan for the same reason. But I cannot be one and the others at the same time. What I can be is myself because I cannot contribute to empowering students when I am ashamed and guilty of my own race. I would caution teachers to avoid placing themselves or their students in vacuum-sealed containers. Certainly our backgrounds, appearances, cultures, and orientations are part of our identities, but we are also individuals. From my own experience, my best strategy has been to get to know people and learn from them. This helps me when I interact with each student. I hope this demonstrates to my students that I value them. Students who are valued feel empowered. At the same time, I make it clear to students that I have high expectations and that I do not accept work that does not meet the standards. However, it is important to be explicit about the criteria for success on any given assignment while providing support to students so they can meet the criteria.

I believe that my story has several implications for teachers. Among them are the need to: increase culturally responsive pedagogy, clarify and expand multicultural teacher education, challenge current hiring practices, and develop mutually caring relationships among staff and students.

Culturally Responsive Teaching

One of the ways in which teachers can contribute to enhancing the academic performance of minority students and English language learners is by engaging them in instruction that is culturally responsive (Trumbull & Pacheco, 2005). Gay (2000), one of the leading proponents of culturally responsive teaching, explains that this type of instruction involves the act of filtering content and strategies through students' cultural lenses to make it meaningful to them; the goal is to improve students' academic achievement while preserving their cultural identity. In addition, culturally responsive pedagogy is a means to transform schools. Culturally responsive educators have the "courage to dismantle the status quo" (Gay, 2000, p. 13).

In my classroom, the notion of culturally responsive teaching is implemented when I have my students read materials that are relevant to their experiences. For example, because many of my students feel that their experiences are not reflected in those of the mainstream culture, I have them compare and contrast two poems with contrasting views of America: Walt Whitman's "I Hear America Singing" and Langston Hughes's "I, Too, Sing America." Central to the poems is the depiction of what could be considered to be two different countries--one in which people seem to be happy and united (Whitman's poem) and the other in which there is inequality (Hughes' poem).

Another way in which I implement culturally responsive teaching is by giving my students a choice in the materials to read. This is done in order to promote student responsibility. For example, in my class, students are given the option to read a short story that is part of our received curriculum, or an alternative such as Sandra Cisneros's

(1991) *The House on Mango Street* or *The Best Short Stories by Black Writers, 1899-1967: The Classic Anthology* (Hughes, 1967). If students do not like any of the choices, we have a class library that has books from authors representing different ethnicities, cultures, and languages. The point is that students decide what they read.

Another critical aspect of culturally responsive teaching, as implemented in my classroom, involves the idea of valuing students' resources while deliberately teaching students standard English so they have access to society's privileges (Delpit, 2006a). As noted by Delpit (2006b), learning standard English will not guarantee student access to society's privileges; however, lack of knowledge of standard English will "almost certainly guarantee failure" (p. 94). A teacher and educational consultant, Mary Berger, trains educators on a practical, step-by-step process that encourages "bidialectalism," the ability to communicate in two dialects. The first step of the training involves proving to students that their home language dialects are rooted in rule-driven "standard" languages (M. Berger, personal communication, July 10, 2007). Berger continues with systematic practice of the two forms: school dialect and friend dialect.[4] The process could certainly be characterized as culturally responsive since it draws on the students' home dialect as a resource that can be used in learning standard English, the school dialect.

---

[4]Delpit (2006b) provides examples of how teachers can implement instruction in standard English, while at the same time, promote the maintenance of the students' home dialect. These examples include engaging students in drama activities in which they use standard English as a means to develop language fluency (rather than accuracy) and asking students to critique their own work (through the use of videos). Other activities include having young learners do puppet shows and role plays of cartoon characters. More recently, Reyes (2010) provides a review of the research on language and ethnicity and discusses instructional implications for speakers of AAVE. Suggested activities include reading the work of well-known African American authors and analyzing how they use AAVE and engaging students in Rickford and Rickford's (2000, cited in Reyes, 2010) bidirectional approach to Contrastive Analysis (CA). While CA is meant to focus on similarities and differences between two dialects, in Rickford and Rickford's view, CA should be done in two directions: from AAVE to standard English and from standard English to AAVE. This bidirectional approach contributes to promoting an understanding of the legitimacy of non-standard dialects.

Teacher Education and Hiring Practices

My story has implications for teacher education and hiring practices. As I described in the opening scenario, the multicultural education classes I have taken for my credential, master's degree, and in my doctoral studies, have certainly helped raise my awareness of how power structures serve some at the expense of others. On the other hand, multicultural education must be clarified and expanded. Pre-service, in-service, and seasoned teachers need to know what the goals of multicultural education are. It is not enough to simply write the goals in a syllabus or on the agenda at a staff development workshop. Such goals should be explicit and discussed at the outset of any course or training session. Furthermore, multicultural education should focus on awareness as well as action. Bennett's (2001) framework for multicultural education, which includes four clusters—curriculum reform, equity pedagogy, multicultural competence, and social equity—is particularly useful in establishing clarity and purpose for multicultural education.

The results of multicultural education appear promising (Dome et al., 2005; Gay, 2010; Sleeter & Owuor, 2011; Vavrus, 2002); however, the promise is long overdue, and it might be necessary to change hiring practices (Sleeter, 2005). Sleeter argues that "educators of color are much more likely to bring life experiences and viewpoints that critique white supremacy than are white teachers and to engage in activities that challenge various forms of racism" (p. 255). As such, hiring panels should strongly attempt to populate classrooms and administrative offices with people from diverse backgrounds, with the understanding that diversity is more than race. These individuals should be willing to learn from one another and from their students. Staff must be able to critique and challenge society and encourage their students to do so, while simultaneously inspiring them in hopes that our future is more humane and just. In the event that our future falls short of our dreams, however, these teachers must also prepare students for such a reality. Individuals who have faced challenges similar to the ones their students face are excellent role models to emulate. Ultimately, the students themselves should have the strongest voices in deciding who gets hired. They do, after all, have the most at stake, and the future belongs to them. In the end, reform efforts that exclude the voices of the greatest stakeholders, our children, are likely doomed. Indeed, I have selected my words carefully so as not to exclude myself from teaching students of color, for although I will never see myself as the ideal teacher, I can learn to be better, every day.[5]

Caring Relationships

The notion of "caring in the classroom" has recently emerged as an area of growing interest and research in relation to K-12 teaching and learning. Central to this notion is the idea that teachers who care are more effective teachers because they treat students fairly (Garrett, Barr, & Rothman, 2009) and create an emotional student-teacher bond that contributes to higher cognitive student engagement (Hachey, 2012). Caring teachers also work to help students meet their academic and pedagogical needs (Kemp & Reupert, 2012) and engage in "tough" (Noblit, 1993, p. 35) relationships, or relationships in which they exert their authority (Noblit, 1993) and set high student expectations (Gay, 2002) to the point that they have been called "warm demanders" (Bondy & Ross, 2008, p. 54).

I believe that in addition to populating classrooms with individuals who have diverse points of view and life experiences (Sleeter, 2005), attention must be paid to developing caring relationships

[5]As noted by Sleeter and Owuor (2011), most teachers in the U.S. "come from White, female, heterosexual, middle-class backgrounds" (p. 534). While there is a need to hire teachers who are more reflective of the U.S. student population, it is also true that just because teachers share their students' ethnic, racial, or linguistic background does not necessarily mean that they will be better teachers. I believe that teacher education programs can play an important role in preparing all teachers for the implementation of multicultural curricula designed to promote improved student academic performance.

among teachers and students. Without care among individuals in a school (or family or workplace), success is less likely. With respect to teacher-student caring, one article that I read in my master's program stands out: "I Want My Teachers to Like Me" (Tan, 2001). Tan argued that respecting students' cultures leads to student investment in school. Particularly powerful were the voices of the students themselves who wanted their teachers to "like us," "like our culture," "respect us," "respect our language," and "like Mexico" (p. 40). More, Gay (2000) acknowledged that caring teachers empower students and challenge them to achieve academically and find their place in a confusing society.

I hope my story demonstrates that "active relationships based on mutual caring between members of culturally diverse communities" (Raible & Irizarry, 2007, p. 192) have made me a better teacher and a better person. I am thankful to work with coworkers who continue to open my eyes. Just the other day when I asked an African-American coworker to pass me my purse in the car, he hesitated, saying, "I never touch a purse because if something were to come up missing, who's the first person they'd look at?" Conversations like these call my attention to the fact that there are things my colleagues have to think about all the time that I do not have to think about at all, and this compels me to take some responsibility.

Taking responsibility for inequalities implies acknowledging the difference between acceptance and maintenance. I accept the idea that students need to learn standard English for now, but I continue to challenge the notion that one variety of a language is better than another. I often find myself in awkward positions at curricular revision meetings or on hiring panels, wondering if the argument I am making is going to cost me my job, particularly when the fog of denial moves in. In these moments, amidst the fog, I see clearly for a moment, but then I begin to struggle again, fearing for my job for what I say and what I do not say, for who I am and for who I can never be. In these moments, I am caught in an unforgivable hesitation. In the end, it is up to the reader to determine whether I can be trusted.

Searching for a Linguistic Community: A Call for the Recognition of Multilingual and Multicultural Identities

SHANNON LADYMON
Maebashi City Board of Education, Japan

Humans are social animals by nature and therefore need to belong to a community. However, the difficulty for me has come in finding exactly which community that is—the one that I can belong to and call my own. The difficulties of a childhood split between states combined with a strong desire to be accepted led me on a long journey to find a linguistic community where I could fit in. Only with age and experience was I able to come to terms with my linguistic identity and assert my rights as a member of multiple communities. This narrative details my experiences as well as calls for a recognition for the membership rights of others.

Growing Up as an Outsider

I am, perhaps, the quintessential American. My ancestry includes two immigrant great-grandfathers, one from Germany and one from Mexico, and numerous other "non-immigrant" (or truthfully, earlier immigrant) ancestors that can be traced back to the American Revolution. Physically, I take after my German and English sides, blending in easily as a white American. Culturally and linguistically, my background is varied. However, in true American fashion, most of the diversity was diluted by the overwhelming standardizing effect of intervening generations so that I grew up reasonably monoculturally and monolinguistically. As the 13th generation on my father's side to be born in Dallas, Texas, I was set up perfectly for the life of a typical American.

Yet, something went wrong. Although my white skin, blond hair, English language, and upper-middle-class socioeconomic status predicted that I would easily fit in with American circles, the reality turned out to be somewhat different. The main problem was one of community. My parents were divorced when I was an infant and had split custody, which became a distinct barrier to forming community bonds when my mother moved to California right before I began school. This effectively severed any close ties I had to friends my age in Texas and also left me in a period of adjustment right as I began school. I stood out because of my accent at first, although I quickly learned that this was something that ought to be controlled and adapted.

Unfortunately, my accent was not something that could just be changed one time and left alone. Instead, each summer I would spend two months in Texas, socializing with relatives and neighbors and trying to find friends to play with. Each summer I would redevelop my Texan accent, only to find it a disability when I came back to California and started school again each fall. The Texan accent would fade as I associated with my Californian classmates, but the process was a constant struggle that would repeat itself each year. I clearly remember one incident where I spent ten minutes in class trying to say the word *crayon* without having anyone understand me because I pronounced it as *crown*. I had thought I had mainly mastered my accent by that point, but the laughter and teasing of my classmates showed me that I had not.

This story exemplifies some of the difficulties I faced fitting in to my new Californian community. As Hansen (2004) has noted, most people assume that if you look like them, you must not have to struggle to fit in with them. I looked very similar to my Californian peers, but I was not like them. I came from a different place entirely and was unsure of how to fit in. I scrambled to assimilate as quickly as possible but never quite felt like I truly belonged; it was all an attempt to fit in, not a valid sense of belonging. Wherever I went, I adapted my dialect, my body language, my actions, and anything else I possibly could in order to seem like I fit in. Kim (2003) has described this context-dependent identity shifting as "identity 'masking" (p. 155), a form of cultural and social adaptation used to hide involvement with unaccepted languages and cultures and to exploit involvement with those language and cultures that are accepted and admired.

The talent that I had developed for using linguistic devices to become a community member (since physically I could easily pass for one without adaptation) became one of my defining characteristics. I began to vary my language not only for survival but also for entertainment. I can remember various stages I went through, trying out personas to see how they felt: the valley girl, the strong man with an Austrian accent, or even the cowboy with the drawl. Each was yet another linguistic mask that I experimented with, attempting to find the true me.

Searching for a Community

My fascination with linguistic variation did not decrease as I grew older. Instead, my interest in language increased. In junior high, I began studying Spanish. I loved Spanish and even won an award for the most outstanding Spanish student in my junior high. I decided I wanted more. In my freshman year of high school, I enrolled in Latin. Again, I was enthralled by learning the language—the rules, the forms, the patterns. I switched back to Spanish the next year, but again, did not stick with it. Instead, something life-altering intervened: Japanese.

Although I had been searching for a linguistic community to belong to for most of my life, the exchange year I spent in Japan when I was sixteen was perhaps the most painful attempt I have made to fit in. I went to Japan without knowing how to say more than *hello* and *thank you* in Japanese. I went to Japan with some knowledge of Japanese culture gleaned from a few books but no true knowledge of what culture shock entails. I left Japan in love with the Japanese language, culture, and country, but devastated by the knowledge that to the community I most wanted to belong, I would forever be considered an outsider. Despite the fluency I developed while in Japan, I would regularly be frustrated in my attempts to use the language or fit into Japanese society. Store clerks and new acquaintances would automatically assume I could not understand Japanese and would use broken English with me even when I initiated conversations in Japanese. Similarly, I was often given forks instead of chopsticks, bread instead of rice, a chair instead of a seat on the ground, and many other accommodations for my foreignness when I desperately wanted nothing more than to simply be treated the same as everyone else. I was constantly aware that I was seen as incapable of fitting in. Liu (2004) expressed clearly what I experienced when he wrote that "social identity sometimes requires mutual acceptance" (p. 29). It is such a simple statement, but it hides the immense difficulty that individuals face admitting its truth.

I came back to the United States feeling as if I belonged to the Japanese community, wanting to speak Japanese, act Japanese, and be Japanese, but knowing that no one would accept me as such. It could be argued that the idea that I could possibly be part of the Japanese linguistic community was unacceptable to both Japanese and Americans because of the general public's dominant view of a "singular, exclusive and oppositional notion of linguistic identity—we must have one linguistic identity *or* the other, we cannot have both" (May, 2005, p. 337, italics in original). Although this was not how I viewed identity, it was laughable to Japanese and American people that I could think I was in any way Japanese, when I obviously (in their minds) was not. Whether I spoke Japanese seemed to have no bearing on the situation or on their perceptions of my linguistic identity. Kubota and Lin (2006) have noted that this is often the case when people's linguistic identities are at odds with the stereotypical linguistic identities associated with their race or physical appearance.

As mentioned, I am, to all appearances, the quintessential American. This means that despite who I might feel I am, others will insist on viewing me as monocultural and monolingual (Hansen, 2004). When I returned from Japan, I began to fight against the prevalent views that people held about my identity. No longer did I struggle to simply fit in with whatever community I currently resided in. Instead,

I fought to be accepted as someone who was more than she appeared. I fought to be accepted as a multicultural, multilingual individual who had a valid claim to whichever languages and cultures she chose. Kanno and Norton (2003) have described this as having an "imagined community," where individuals construct their identities through imagining themselves as a part of the communities to which they believe they should belong, and thereby "expand [their] range of possible selves" (p. 246). Reconceptualizing my identity by throwing away my previous limited understanding of the identity possibilities—the dichotomy of either American or Japanese—opened new and empowering doors for me as a multilingual, just as it has done for many nonnative speakers of English (Pavlenko, 2003).

To assert my multilingualism, I took as many language classes as possible once I entered college—Hebrew, Korean, German, Japanese, and Spanish. I made as many friends from other countries as I could and attended as many cultural gatherings as I had access to. I still strongly remember being invited to my Dutch-Israeli friend's home for Passover, where his family conducted the entire ceremony in Hebrew while I did my best to participate. It did not matter to me that I was neither perfectly fluent nor perfectly culturally knowledgeable. As long as I was allowed, I would claim whatever membership I could.

I am finally coming to terms with my identity. After graduating from college, I began my work on a master's degree in TESOL. The classes that I took and the articles and books I read in graduate school reinforced my understanding of who I am. Norton and Toohey (2001) have argued that language learners must fight to be viewed as rightful participants in a linguistic community in order to re-form their identities. This is what I have attempted. From a young age, I have been in search of a linguistic community to call my own; finally, I have given up the search and created my own. My linguistic community is the sum of all the communities that I claim membership to, none of which I have a "real" claim to but all of which I insist on participating in as a rightful member. I may not understand perfectly, but I listen to Korean music with my Korean friends, participate in German conversations with my German friends, make phone calls in Japanese with my Japanese friends, watch Indian movies in Tamil with my Indian friends, and chat at coffee shops in English with my North American friends. I am not limited to an English only, North American only experience simply because of my ethnicity or nationality. My identity is plain and simply *me*, in all my forms.

Integrating Instruction on Identity Issues in the Language Classroom

The world we live in is becoming increasingly globalized, with people from many different backgrounds at many different stages of life experiencing the difficulties of learning other languages. I have numerous friends and acquaintances who have fought to be accepted as English speakers, ranging from those who came to the United States as adolescents and still feel unable to claim full rights to English to those who studied English as a foreign language and cannot conceive of speaking with a native English speaker on equal footing. These examples strike a sympathetic note in me and require action.

As a member of the TESOL community, I believe that it is crucial that we consider the effect of identity crises on language learners. Just as I experienced, learners may struggle to find their place in the world of linguistic communities when they no longer clearly belong to any particular one. They may feel inadequate because of linguistic limitations (Liu, 2004) or may be unaware of their right to speak (Peirce, 1995) and, therefore, longingly hover at the edges of new linguistic communities without knowing how to enter them. I strongly agree with Kim's (2003) view that "the teaching and learning of English is far more complicated than mere questions of using effective techniques, teaching materials and processes" (p. 157). As teachers of English, an increasingly global language, we especially need to encourage our learners to challenge the current power structures, which authors such as Burns (2005) have shown to exclude language learners from ownership of English. Our learners have a right to English, a right to participation, and a right to belong. No individual should be made to feel excluded because she is new to a community—all people have a right to be accepted.

To promote such an understanding of linguistic identity and belonging, I suggest that instructors follow a three-step approach to addressing linguistic identity in the classroom: promote understanding, increase awareness, and encourage ownership.

Promote Understanding

Help your learners understand that identity is dynamic. Identity is dependent on context (Holmes, 2001; Liu, 2004; Peirce, 1995), and learners should be encouraged to explore which identities they have in which contexts. This can be done through a variety of classroom activities at a variety of levels.

- *Beginning levels.* Introduce the idea of multiple identities through topics such as family relationships. Just as someone can be grandmother, mother, aunt, sister, cousin, and daughter at the same time, each of us plays many roles and has many identities depending on who we are interacting with. Expand this discussion to other relationships, such as teacher, friend, neighbor, and more. Tree diagrams or network webs using pictures or drawings of people that students know can serve as an engaging and hands-on activity to explore this.
- *Intermediate levels.* Learners can perform role-plays to show how they would act in different situations with different people. Use lessons about formality (e.g., Mr. Smith versus Bob) and politeness (e.g., *please, sorry*) as a springboard into discussions about how we relate based on power relationships and familiarity and how our identity changes based on those same factors.

- *Advanced levels.* Learners can use journals (such as in Peirce, 1995) to record their experiences in different contexts or even free-writes to discover their inner thoughts and feelings regarding the multiplicity of their identities. These can then be developed into class discussions, oral presentations, or even papers on the topic of how context-dependent identity is.

Increase Awareness

Increase awareness in your learners of the relationship between language usage and identity. Social relationships, as well as other contextual factors, play a large role in determining how language is used (Holmes, 2001). Learners can discover useful ways of controlling their English usage to show the identity they wish to have others perceive. Instructors can bring in videos, audio clips, or written documents demonstrating interactions between people with different social identities and analyze them as a class to discover which forms people used to signal particular identities. Some suggestions for using this technique at different levels are given.

- *Beginning levels.* Play bingo or have a scavenger hunt for words that show identity markers. For example, watch clips from a movie or television show in which certain types of identities and relationships are shown (e.g., boss/subordinate, mother/child, nice person/mean person) and ask students to check off words that show identity on their bingo chart or scavenger list as they hear them. These can be words or phrases like *sir, dear, excuse me, no way, like, totally,* or any others that show the types of identities in your clip. After students have checked these off, go through as a class and talk about which words belong to which identity. This can also be done looking at comics or other types of media.

- *Intermediate levels.* Watch clips from movies or television shows in which the main characters must change their identities. For example, movies where the main characters lie about their jobs and tell their parents or friends or dates that they are lawyers or doctors but in reality they have less prestigious jobs. Alternatively, movies where the main character switches gender (man pretending to be a woman, or woman pretending to be a man). In these clips, ask learners to watch for how the characters' speech changes depending on which identity they assume. Ask students to make a two-column list with words and phrases they heard the character use as one personality and as the other. Then go over this as a class and discuss why certain words or linguistic features were used with one identity as opposed to the other.
- *Advanced levels.* Use excerpts from novels with dialogue to show how people's language use is depicted. This can be especially fruitful with authors who depict nonstandard language forms (e.g., southern dialect) that are markedly different in text. Analyze how the characters in novels speak and how that relates to their identity. This can also be done with other types of non-fiction writing, such as looking at the differences between the vocabulary and grammar used in more academic writing (e.g., textbook, newspaper article) and more popular writing (e.g., online blog, magazine article) and relating these differences to the identities of the writers and their social contexts.

Encourage Ownership

Encourage learners to assert their rights to language ownership. Learners must take an active role in defining their identities as rightful members of linguistic communities in order to be accepted (Norton & Toohey, 2001; Peirce, 1995). Learners should be allowed to explore their linguistic identity and assert their ownership through a variety of classroom activities.

- *Beginning levels.* Although English is the focus of your classroom, change the traditional view of one-language-only and make a game of code-switching that embraces multilingualism. Ask students to get in groups of three, with one student speaking in the first language, a second student acting as interpreter, and a third student speaking in English. This requires that at least two students in each group speak the same language, although the third student needs only to speak English. The student who acts as interpreter will get to use both languages at the same time and show multicompetence. This can be done at beginner levels by having very basic conversations such as introducing oneself, which will still require interpretation.
- *Intermediate levels.* In mixed-language classrooms, ask learners to make presentations to the class about their first languages. This puts them in the position of knowledgeable expert about a language and will encourage reflection about the complexities and difficulties in learning all languages. Discuss the difficulties that English learners might have acquiring those languages, and point out that everyone struggles at first to learn a new language (not just English). In single-language class-

rooms, this can be done by having students present on specific aspects of the first language, such as a grammatical feature. Additionally, if access is available, learners can interview English speakers about their experiences learning foreign languages and report to the class on the difficulties all learners face.

- *Advanced levels.* Assign learners projects that require them to interact with English speakers. In particular, assign projects that put learners in a position of power when interacting with English speakers, such as that of interviewer or customer. As an interviewer or customer, learners can approach English-speaking employees (of a school or business) with a set of questions that they have come up with. For example, a learner may approach a school receptionist and interview him or her on policies of enrollment or attendance. Alternatively, a learner may enter an electronics store, if access is available, and make requests of the store clerk, such as to see a particular DVD player advertised on television or ask for details about a particular product. Such assignments will require learners to embrace English as a tool that they use to accomplish certain goals and thereby help empower them as English speakers.

Through this three-step approach, instructors can bring the discussion of identity and linguistic ownership to the classroom within the context of English-learning activities. Such critical thinking will empower students and enable them to approach learning English with more awareness and sensitivity to the social roles and power structures inherent in language usage.

As language teachers, we have more opportunities than any other group to influence the development of linguistic identity in our students. We should take advantage of such opportunities and foster a sense of linguistic belonging for all of our students so that they may accept their different linguistic identities rather than struggle with them. It is important to integrate activities that will allow learners to understand, explore, and assert ownership over all their linguistic identities, both in their first language(s) and English. These activities can be integrated into lessons with other goals, such as practicing discussion and interview skills, learning politeness features, or listening to recordings for specific information. The important idea to remember is that identity should be explored and discussed rather than dismissed as if irrelevant.

Reflection Question

As explained in this chapter, one does not need to be a native speaker of a language or dialect in order to feel ownership of it. Consider a second language or dialect you speak. To what extent do you feel ownership of it? In what ways is this ownership manifested? And what kind of classroom activities could you implement in order to help students take ownership of the language or dialect being taught?

CHAPTER 4

Beyond Individual Stories and on to the Classroom: Pedagogical Practices that Reflect the Teachers' Identities

Are there any pedagogical practices you implement that reflect your language learning and life learning experiences?

This chapter provides a summary of the pedagogical practices that were identified across the various narratives presented in this book.[1] The chapter also contextualizes the pedagogical practices in current SLA thinking. The chapter concludes with a personal reflection.

"How can I use your experiences to help my second language learners succeed?" As you will recall, this was the question that prompted me to write this book. As I explained, the question was asked at a CATESOL conference presentation after an elementary school teacher—an immigrant from El Salvador to the U.S.—presented her autobiographical narrative. While narratives are not designed to

[1]A particularity of this chapter is that I refer to the autobiography writers by their first name only. I do this to humanize their classrooms.

result in what Johnson (2006) calls "generalized principles of what works" (p. 242), it is clear that the teachers whose narratives are contained in this book implement instruction that is affected by their lived experiences, their values and beliefs, and by the sociocultural and sociopolitical contexts in which they operate. In doing this, they implement pedagogy that they believe will be effective.

In this chapter, the teachers' narratives are re-examined to explore the pedagogical practices implemented by the teachers and to contextualize them within current SLA thinking. My intention is to help readers understand how the teachers' identities inform their pedagogical practices. However, as I explained earlier, one should be cautious since there is not a one-to-one relationship between the teachers' identities and their pedagogical practices. For example, as I explained in Chapter 1, the fact that a teacher is bilingual may not necessarily result in the teacher's adoption of code-switching as an instructional strategy. Alternatively, the fact that a teacher is monolingual may not necessarily result in that same teacher preventing students from using their home languages in the classroom (as shown in Valerie's narrative). Still, it is clear that the teachers' experiences, values, and beliefs have shaped (and continue to shape) their pedagogical practices. Five pedagogical practices that the teachers' narratives highlight are discussed.

◆ Pedagogical Practice Number 1: Teachers Code-Switch in the Language Classroom

One of the commonalities across the narratives is that rather than looking at the students' home language as a problem that needs to be avoided in the classroom, the teachers view the students' L1 as a resource, and use it in the classroom. This view of the role of the L1 in the language classroom is in contrast to a traditional view of second language acquisition that opposes code-switching—alternating between the use of two languages or dialects in the same situation (Kamwangamalu, 2010) in the classroom on the grounds that it interferes with the SLA process (Auerbach, 1993; Canagarajah, 1999; Scott & de la Fuente, 2008). In this view, the English language is better learned monolingually, an idea that several researchers do not support (e.g., Auerbach, 1993; Canagarajah, 1999; Cook, 2001; Levine, 2011). As explained by Liu, Ahn, Baek, and Han (2004), several teaching methodologies (e.g., the direct method, natural approach, total physical response) and approaches (communicative language teaching) emphasize the importance of providing students with English-only input as a means to immerse students in the target language. In contrast, proponents of the use of the L1 in the classroom argue that using it contributes to enhancing L2 learning, promotes more time-efficient learning, and teaches students how to use code-switch strategically, a skill that is necessary in multilingual situations (Liu, Ahn, Baek, & Han, 2004). Additionally, researchers like Levine (2011) argue that if one accepts the premise that code-switching involves dynamic and creative processes, then the use of more than one language in the classroom cannot be perceived as a problem since adult L2 learners usually have access to and use more than one code (Levine, 2011).

The teachers' narratives show that teachers code-switch for two different purposes: to reduce the cognitive load and to teach students how to use languages strategically. Hee-Jin's narrative provides examples of how code-switching can contribute to lowering the language learners' cognitive load. Specifically, on those instances in which Hee Jin knows the students' L1, she implements a three-step approach to introducing new ideas or grammatical concepts: (1) she uses Korean to explain a new idea; (2) she uses English to reinforce the idea previously introduced in Korean; and (3) she uses English again for practice purposes. For example, Hee-Jin introduces the present perfect tense in Korean, reintroduces the present perfect tense in English, and finally uses the English language to provide students with opportunities to practice the present perfect tense. This three-step approach to instruction may allow students to learn the English language efficiently since it promotes the understanding of concepts faster than if an English-only approach had been implemented.

Angel's narrative also supports the notion of code-switching based on her own experience as a second language learner in the Philipines where one of her teachers punished students by fining them every time that they did not use English. Angel is convinced this strategy harms language learners, particularly those at the beginning level, since they do not have enough vocabulary to communicate solely in English. Therefore, she argues that avoiding code-switching would result in poor instruction. To avoid this problem, Angel creates a classroom environment in which language learners see their peers as resources. She allows students to rely on the resources their peers bring to the classroom by asking them to translate vocabulary or ideas into their L1. I should add that while Angel is a strong proponent of code-switching, she also opposes its use if she sees that students are code-switching with the purpose of alienating some of their peers or creating in-groups. This may be the case of students who share an L1 and, because they code-switch extensively to communicate among themselves, make other students uncomfortable or alienated. In this case, Angel has what she calls "a zero tolerance attitude" and requires that students switch to English.

Often times, the use of code-switching is associated with monolingual classrooms. What is informative about Angel's use of code-switching is that she works with multilingual groups, so it would be impossible for her to know or speak all of her students' L1. For this reason, Angel can't act as a resource in most cases. Her students have to fulfill the role of "informants." It can be argued that playing such a role provides an unexpected or unintentional benefit since students learn how to negotiate information in multilingual settings, a skill they will most probably need to rely on in a globalized world.

Much like Angel, Valerie, a white teacher who works with bidialectical African-American and Latino students who are Spanish speakers, does not speak Spanish, some of her students' L1. However, in contrast to Angel, who does not view her inability to use her students' languages as a problem, Valerie expresses deep concern about her lack of Spanish skills since they prevent her from creating stronger bonds with her Spanish-speaking students. Rather than forbidding the use of the students' home language, a strategy that would deny students access to valuable class information, Valerie relies on a bilingual teaching assistant who acts as a language broker for the whole class. The teaching assistant plays a central role in Valerie's classroom since it is his knowledge of English and Spanish that allows Valerie to create a learning community that, without the teaching assistant's participation, would be more difficult to create.

Shannon's narrative also proposes the use of code-switching in a group activity in which at least two students speak the same language. Specifically, she puts her students in groups of three in which one student speaks the L1 only, the second student acts as the interpreter, and the third student speaks English only. This is a good example of how code-switching can be used to embrace the notion of multilingualism and to teach students how they can alternate the use of the L1 and L2 in multilingual settings.

It is clear that Hee-Jin, Angel, Valerie, and Shannon view code-switching as a positive instructional strategy. At the same time, the teachers' beliefs about code-switching and their use of code-switching in the classroom provide information on how the teachers perceive their identities, vis-à-vis those of their students. Specifically, when Hee-Jin works with Korean students, with whom she shares her L1 and cultural background, she positions herself as an insider to the community in which her students belong. This self-perception contributes to strengthening the teacher-student relationship, ultimately promoting a sense of classroom community. Angel, Shannon, and Valerie reflect somewhat different realities. Angel, a bilingual speaker who works in a multilingual setting, does not see her inability to use her students' languages as a problem; for her, the problem would be enforcing an only-English language policy since it would prevent students from accessing content. Angel's self-perception as a bilingual or multicompetent speaker allows her to see herself in a positive light vis-à-vis her students, which contributes to a sense of comfort about her position in the classroom. Much like Angel, Shannon is multilingual and multicultural. She believes that in a globalized world, it is critical that teachers prepare students to use the resources they bring to the classroom, and one of these resources is their home language. Valerie's case is completely different from those of her colleagues. Valerie is white and does not speak Spanish. Her narrative shows that she questions her role as a teacher; her being white contributes to feelings of insecurity and guilt and position Valerie as an outsider to the students' community. While one could question the degree of effectiveness of a teacher who feels insecure and guilty; I believe it is the very questioning of her own status that leads Valerie to identify pedagogical practices that are designed to meet her students' academic and affective needs. One of the practices she has identified is relying on a bilingual teaching assistant who acts as a language broker. Therefore, one can see that rather than controlling the classroom setting by preventing students from using their L1, Valerie creates an environment that values the students' L1 and helps them see it as a resource.

While all of the narrative authors strongly support the role that the L1 plays in the L2 classroom, the use of code-switching in the classroom could go one step further. Levine (2011) argues that the use of code-switching in the classroom should integrate what he calls "critical reflection" (p. 100). Central to this notion is the idea that the integration of code-switching in the language classroom needs to get students to make conscious, rather than unconscious, decisions about code-switching. In order to reach this goal, students should participate in a variety of activities that asks them to reflect on what language or code they would use under different circumstances and the reasons why they would use such languages or codes. For example, one such activity involves asking students to compare communication in the classroom with communication "in the real world" (Levine, 2011, p. 133). Specifically, working in pairs or groups, students create two lists—one identifying the language(s) they use outside the classroom (e.g., at the coffee shop, the bank, etc.) and the other identifying the language(s) they use inside the classroom. After tallying the responses for the whole class, students discuss the language choices associated with each of the two settings and the reasons for such choices. Finally, students can reflect on their learning from the activity and, more specifically, discuss the implications of their learning for their language classroom. This type of activity, involving reflection, results in language learner awareness about the various roles that languages play in their lives.

◆ Pedagogical Practice Number 2: Teachers Draw on their Own Identities as a Means to Create Classroom Communities

Classrooms in which students feel part of a community create positive learning conditions. In recent years, researchers and practitioners have legitimately argued that teachers from a nonnative English–speaking background can create classroom communities by drawing on their nonnative identities (Amin, 1997; 2004; Braine, 1999). Amin (2004) further argues that NNESTs who are visible minorities promote trust because they disrupt the myth of the native speaker of English as being white (though she also notes that visible minorities don't fit the stereotype of the "native speaker" so their professional competence may be initially questioned). They also serve as excellent role models for their students. Like their students, these teachers had to learn the L2 and in ESL settings their experiences may reflect those of their students, that is, they may have gone through an immigration process or overcome many obstacles (Auerbach, 1993).

Several narratives support the idea that NNESTs can create positive learning conditions because they share many of their students' experiences and have a first-hand understanding of their students' struggles, needs, and successes. Jessie's narrative makes reference to the benefits NNESTs bring to the classroom. Growing up, Jessie's language learning experience was made traumatic by the challenges she faced as a U.S. immigrant and ethnic minority. In her narrative, Jessie argues that because teachers from an ethnic and linguistic minority background have often been marginalized, they, in turn, are more likely to develop the ability to construct classroom environments that promote empowerment for marginalized students. This can be done by actively supporting bilingual (or multilingual) policies and by helping L2 learners who may be going through a turbulent/traumatic process of learning the target language or adapting to U.S. culture. Teachers from an ethnic and linguistic minority background can also create classroom communities because they understand the conflicts learners may face about their L1 and L2 cultures. Therefore, they are adept at mitigating such conflict and promote what Jessie calls "a peaceful classroom environment."

Jeremy draws on his identity as a speaker of a regional dialect, Southern American English, in order to create classroom communities. In so doing, Jeremy challenges the notion that there is only one variety of English, the one that is typically used in classroom books and tapes. After struggling with how he perceived himself for several years, Jeremy now views the variety of English that he grew up with, and which still influences his speech, as different (rather than deficient) from the many other "Englishes" of the world. Most importantly, Jeremy draws on his experience as a tool to enhance his students' learning experiences.

Jeremy's experience is valuable in two ways. First, it supports the notion that that we should avoid making generalizations about teachers, just as we should avoid making generalizations about language learners. Kubota and Lin (2006) very eloquently argue that the TESOL field has tended to associate whiteness with standard English and native speaker status and non-whiteness with nonnative speaker status, which has led to overgeneralizing and disregarding the experiences of teachers who "do not fit this formula" (Kubota & Lin, 2006, p. 481). The second reason Jeremy's experience is valuable is because it shows that one does not need to be an ethnic minority in order to be able to create classroom communities. Teachers can draw on their life experiences as a means to identify commonalities with their students that could inform their instructional practices.

It is not challenging for teachers to create communities when teachers share commonalities with their students. However, a frequent question is how can teachers create communities when they don't have much in common with their students? This is the case of Valerie, who still questions her role as "a white teacher" after years of teaching at the same school. Reading the work by Peirce (1995) helped Valerie understand how important it is to develop a professional identity that draws on one's strengths, which Valerie did.

As I noted in Chapter 1, the notion of caring was new to me when I first read Valerie's narrative. In fact, initially, I attributed the idea of caring to Valerie's concern about her own status as a white teacher who did not have much in common with her students. However, after reviewing the literature on the topic, I realized that the notion of caring has received growing attention in the K-12 literature over the last few years (e.g., Bondy & Ross, 2008; Garrett, Barr, & Rothman, 2009; Gay, 2002; Hachey, 2012; Kemp & Reupert, 2012; Noblit, 1993). The notion of caring goes well beyond what Gay (2002) refers to as "gentle nurturing and altruistic concern" (p. 109). Teachers like Valerie, that is, teachers who care, are considered to be "tough" (Noblit, 1993, p. 35) or "warm demanders" (Bondy & Ross, 2008, p. 54). The reason for this is that they have very high student expectations, while, at the same time, provide support so that students meet such expectations. And this is accomplished "without ignoring, demeaning, or neglecting their ethnic and cultural identities" (Gay, 2002, p. 110).

◆ Pedagogical Practice Number 3: Teachers Integrate Instruction in Varieties of English

Several of the narratives argue that language learners should be given exposure to different varieties of English. This practice is supported by two rationales. The first is that students need to become aware that speaking a dialect that is different from standard American English does not equal deficiency. The second is to create awareness of the many varieties of English used within the U.S. and around the world.

The belief that language learners need to be exposed to World Englishes is consistent with a view of instruction that is in opposition to a monocentric view of the English language (Quirk, 1990, as cited in Jenkins, 2006, p. 171). In this view, the only acceptable standard is a native speaker from an Inner Circle country. Currently, English is perceived as an international language (Matsuda, 2012), and with its global spread, it has resulted in many different varieties that differ from those of Inner Circle countries (see Kachru & Smith, 2008; Matsuda, 2012). In contrast to a monocentric framework, in which only one standard is acceptable, what is appreciated from a World Englishes perspective is "the variation and cultural pluralism denoted by the term 'Englishes'" (Kachru & Smith, 2008, p. 4). While Jeremy, Angel, and Valerie are concerned about teaching their students SAE, they work, at the same time, to make their students aware that there are many Englishes. At the same time, Valerie and Jessie, who teach in K–12 settings in California are concerned about showing their students that their home languages are valued and that their bilingualism is a source of strength. I believe that this concern can be attributed not only to the teachers' beliefs about languages, but also to their reaction toward current language policies in California, which, with the passing of Proposition 227 in 1998 dismantled most bilingual education programs in the state and required California schools to implement English-only classes. Such a draconian policy has resulted in classrooms where language learners are prevented from using their home language, thereby promoting in students a sense of shame since they are led to believe that their home language is a problem.

Jeremy, who teaches adult ESL learners, takes the view that in their everyday lives, his immigrant students will be exposed to many different varieties of English spoken in the United States. Therefore, in his class, instruction in language variation is designed to accomplish two goals. First, it is meant to help his students understand that their accented English represents a variety of English that is different from the one spoken by other people in their community. In doing this, Jeremy's goal is to make his students aware that their English is not deficient, but simply different. The second goal in integrating instruction in language variation is to help his students understand how English is used in their community. This allows students to hear how language is used for real purposes and to see how "non-standard, shortened, and ungrammatical everyday speech can be."

In order to accomplish the two goals, Jeremy engages his students in a variety of activities, two of which are highlighted here. The first one involves exposing students to speakers of World Englishes through recordings or classroom visits followed by class discussions about the meaning of terms like *native* and *nonnative English speaker*. The second activity engages students in role-play activities in which they are made aware that decisions about the language or dialect used in a conversation are not random but are instead tied to various factors including, but not limited to, their (or their interlocutors') degree of proficiency in English—issues of gender, class, power, and ethnicity, as well as the purpose of the conversation.

Angel also values the idea of language variation. Angel does not see herself as a nonnative speaker of English because it would position her as a fossilized learner rather than a sophisticated English language user. Therefore, drawing on Cook's (1999) notion of multicompetence, she chooses to see herself as a multicompetent English language user. This positioning has a strong impact on what happens in her classroom because it allows her to see herself and students in a positive light by embracing multilingualism and code-switching as positive classroom strategies. Whenever possible, she emphasizes the notion that intelligible L2 users are successful models to emulate rather than fossilized nonnative speakers (Cook, 1999).

Valerie's narrative also emphasizes the value of linguistic diversity. This is done by teaching students that their home dialects are "rule-driven." She also introduces the idea of bidialectalism by making students aware of the differences between two dialects, "the language of school" (academic, standard) and "the language of friends" (colloquial, non-standard). This reveals to students how they can deliberately use the two dialects to access different opportunities.

This view embraces the resources that students bring to the classroom and, at the same time, gives them access to SAE. In fact, this view places great emphasis on helping students value their bilingualism or bidialectism. I should note that while Valerie's strategy is designed to send the message that the students' home language and dialect are legitimate, the fact that English or standard English are presented as "the language of school" will lead her students to compartmentalize their use and perceive English and standard English as the language of power. In this case, I believe that Rickford and Rickford's bidirectional approach to CA (as cited in Reyes, 2010) involving the analysis of similarities and differences going in two directions—from non-standard dialects (e.g., AAVE) to standard English and from standard English to AAVE—would contribute to helping students understand the legitimacy of their home language or dialect. For example, this bidirectional approach could be implemented when Valerie's students read and analyzed the work of authors like Walt Whitman and Langston Hughes.

◆ Pedagogical Practice Number 4: Teachers Promote Culturally Responsive Instruction

The narratives reveal that teachers are concerned about promoting instruction that is culturally responsive. This type of instruction has two underlying rationales. First, culturally responsive instruction is meaningful because it draws on the knowledge that students bring to the classroom and allows them to relate to the content presented (Gay, 2010). In fact, a well-known practice in second language classrooms involves drawing on students' background knowledge as a means to allow them to access new ideas and information (Trumbull & Pacheco, 2005). Second, culturally responsive instruction allows students to see their cultures and topics of interest to them reflected in the school curriculum; therefore, rather than finding the topics of relevance to their lives marginalized, they see people like themselves playing an integral part of the curriculum (Gay, 2010; Sleeter & Owuor, 2011). Ultimately, the two rationales support the goal of enhancing student academic achievement while at the same time, preserving the students' cultural identity.

Culturally responsive instruction goes well beyond the idea of "multicultural week," "diversity week," or the presentation of superficial topics like "typical food in your country, customs in your country, holidays celebrated in your country." As explained by Kasper and Omori (2010), such a focus depicts cultures as being static and monolithic when, in reality, issues of age, religion, gender, etc., contribute to making cultures diverse. At the same time, a focus on topics like those mentioned can position immigrant students as outsiders to the community in which they live. For example, when topics like "typical food or customs in your country" are presented, the message students receive is that they do not belong in "this" country. Therefore, students are put in a position of "the other," a position that promotes an unhealthy identity (Kasper & Omori, 2010). Culturally responsive instruction does not avoid controversial topics but by addressing them, it analyzes individuals, topics, and texts within the context of race and ethnicity, poverty, class, gender, political discourse, etc.

Gay (2002) also argues that culturally responsive instruction is about integrating multicultural content *and* multicultural instructional strategies. While there are many individual differences in how individual members of a particular cultural group act in the classroom (due to issues of gender, class, educational background, age, personality factors, etc.), there is also research that shows that there are some general speech norms and classroom participatory strategies that apply to different cultural groups. In this respect, the pioneering work of Shirley Brice Heath (focusing on an African-American working class community and a white working class community) and Susan Philips (focusing on Native American students in an Indian reservation) (cited in Kasper and Omoni, 2010) need to be highlighted. Their research showed that the mismatches between the socialization practices of the home and the school leads students to have difficulty in school and, at the same time, leads schools to perceive the students' home culture as deficient rather than different. Gay (2002, 2010) argues that teachers who implement culturally responsive instruction are aware of potential home-classroom differences and implement instructional strategies that are congruent with the students' way of communicating. Valerie's narrative provides examples of how she maximizes students' opportunities for learning by drawing on culturally congruent practices.

When making decisions about culturally responsive instruction, teachers need to be careful about overgeneralizations. One cannot assume that just because students are African American, for example, they will speak AAVE, enjoy hip hop music and poetry, and prefer working in groups. The argument that culturally responsive instruction depicts cultures as being diverse and vital also applies to the students who will be exposed to a culturally responsive curriculum.

Valerie's narrative provides examples of how she implements culturally responsive instruction. In her class, Valerie replaces the given curriculum for curriculum that is relevant to her students' lives. For example, she has students read African-American and Latino authors. However, there will be times when the implementation of a culturally relevant curriculum may not be possible. For example, not teaching Shakespeare on the basis that it may not draw on Latino students' background or content knowledge would limit these students' world view and academic preparation. In a case like this, it is important to draw on the universality of the literature being studied. At the same time, students would benefit from instruction designed to help them access the piece of literature and see the relevance of the work being studied to their own lives.

◆ Pedagogical Practice Number 5: Teachers Integrate Instruction in Power Relations and Language Use

Shannon's narrative shows how L2 teachers can integrate explicit instruction in linguistic identity. Her rationale for integrating instruction in linguistic identity relies on the fact that "learners have a right to English, a right to participation, and a right to belong." To achieve this goal, Shannon's approach to instruction involves three steps:

helping students understand that one's identity is dynamic; increasing students' awareness about the relationship between language usage and identity; and encouraging language learners to "assert their rights to language ownership."

Central to Shannon's approach is the notion that language learners should be given opportunities to (1) critically think about the role that social relations play when communicating in English (or the students' L1) and (2) take ownership of the English language so that they can assert their right to speak. Shannon's ideas draw on the work by Peirce (1995), who argues that the SLA theories place too much emphasis on the individual nature of the L2 learning process and depict language learners as people who are "ahistorical and unidimensional" (p. 25), rather than complex individuals whose social identities will change dependent on the social context in whey they have to function. Peirce (1995) also argues that immigrant language learners (and I would add EFL students) have limited opportunities to interact in English outside the classroom, so language teachers need to provide students with such opportunities so that they can take ownership of the language. However, this cannot be accomplished unless language learners understand how language is used in social interaction (Peirce, 1995). It is this very aspect of language use that Shannon addresses in her classes.

The activities that Shannon describes in her narrative--for example, analyzing the register and degree of politeness used in dialogs in different social situations as a springboard to discuss the relationship among language, power relationships, and familiarity--can be considered to be a form of critical literacy. Critical literacy goes well beyond focusing on the development of content knowledge and instead focuses on the idea that education is meant to help learners engage in social action and that, in order for this action to take place, learners need to be able to read the word and the world in a critical manner. These ideas were first discussed by the Brazilian educator Paulo Freire (1990), who argued that the purpose of literacy instruction should be to help the poor challenge the status quo and dismantle the power structures that keep them oppressed. While Shannon's pedagogical practices do not go that far toward the goal of dismantling power structures, they are meant to make her language learners aware that the language they use or the language that is used to communicate with them is not neutral.

◆ Conclusion as Personal Reflection

The pedagogical practices discussed here are not meant to be exhaustive but to provide readers with some practical ideas about how the teachers' lived experiences are reflected in the language classrooms. I hope that readers will identify some of their own pedagogical practices in the discussion and will be prompted to consider how their own personal and professional lives affect their instructional practices.

In reviewing the narratives to identify the teachers' pedagogical practices, I was struck by the fact that running through the narratives was a common theme of "otherness" or "isolation." In fact, all the narratives highlight in some way how the teachers were perceived as "the other" at some point of their professional or personal life. The narratives also highlight the teachers' struggles to overcome such feelings and perceptions (those of others and their own) and to explain how their struggles affected their beliefs about teaching and learning. While readers could gather that I intentionally selected narratives that focused on the theme of "otherness," this is far from the truth. In fact, it was only upon reading and re-reading the narratives that I noticed how strongly this idea came through in the stories. That led me to question why I had selected these particular narratives. After I read an article by Menard-Warwick (2011), I came to the conclusion that, much like her, my own life history, in which I never saw myself quite fitting, is what led me to be particularly sensitive to and interested in the life experiences of professionals who may eventually reach their personal and professional goals but who do so only as a result of a struggle.

I was born and raised in Argentina where I am an invisible minority. I am a member of a minority group because I am Jewish and a

Sephardic Jew—a descendant of Jews whose homeland was Spain and who, at the time of the Spanish Inquisition in 1492, were expelled from the Spanish peninsula (unless they converted to Catholicism).[2] While Jews are active in all levels of Argentine society, we have always perceived ourselves and are perceived as being outsiders in Argentine society. Additionally, it is not uncommon to see swings in societal attitudes toward Jews in Argentina. As noted by the American-Israeli Cooperative Enterprise (2012), "From an open door policy of immigration to the harboring of Nazi war criminals, Argentina's Jews have faced periods of peaceful coexistence and periods of intense anti-semitism." Besides being a member of a minority group, in Argentina, I am an *invisible* minority because my physical appearance makes me fit into mainstream society. I do not "look Jewish" (or I do not look like the stereotypical Jew), so it has not been uncommon for me to hear people make negative comments about Jews to my face because I can "pass." These comments are usually followed by an immediate reaction designed to challenge my interlocutors' ideas. As a result, I believe that it is my own history of perceiving myself and being perceived as "the other" that led me to select the narratives contained in this book.

Reflection Question

What are the pedagogical practices you have read about in this chapter that you can adopt or adapt to implement in your own classroom? What benefits would they bring to your students? Would they bring any challenges? If so, which ones?

---

[2]In Judaism, there are two cultural branches: Ashkenazic Jews (who come from countries like France, Germany, and Eastern Europe) represent the largest majority of Jews. In contrast, Sephardic Jews (who come from Spain, Portugal, and Middle Eastern countries) represent a much smaller group. Therefore, Sephardic Jews are considered to be a minority subgroup within a minority group.

CHAPTER 5

From the Language Classroom to the Teacher Preparation Classroom: Using Narratives to Promote Teacher Reflection

If you are a language teacher educator, what are the advantages and disadvantages of integrating the autobiographical narrative genre into your courses?

"The identity paper was my favorite project in the program and one of the most important things I'll take from this program. Thank you!"

This comment was made by an anonymous Educational Sociolinguistics pre-service teacher on the end-of-the-term student opinion survey in the fall 2010. Some readers may think the statement is self-serving; but I offer it as an example of what my pre-service teachers have had to say about the autobiographical narrative assignment. Over the years, the pre-service teachers in my class have not always had positive things to say about class assignments, but the autobiographical narrative has received comments that were unanimously positive.

This chapter discusses how the assignment is integrated into my TESL 570 Educational Sociolinguistics course, describes assignment expectations, and provides information on the readings pre-service teachers complete in preparation for the assignment. I further describe the assessment criteria used to evaluate the narratives and reflect on the challenges and opportunities provided by the autobiographical narrative assignment.

◆ Assignment Expectations and Course Materials

As part of this assignment, pre-service teachers are required to write five or six pages describing their language learning history and how they think it relates to their beliefs about classroom teaching and learning. If pre-service teachers are already teaching or have teaching experience, then they are asked to reflect on whether there are any potential connections between their current or past instructional practices and their language learning history. The assignment also requires making connections with the literature discussed in class (see Table 1).

To make assignment expectations explicit, I provide pre-service teachers with a checklist of assessment criteria in advance of the assignment deadline (See Figure 1). The checklist was developed in collaboration with past TESL 570 Educational Sociolinguistics classes. The first few times I gave the assignment, the students and I brainstormed the initial assessment criteria. A draft version of the checklist was revised in collaboration with the students of that and future classes. The checklist has continued to evolve over the years.

The materials to which pre-service teachers are exposed are important in promoting critical, alternative discourses (Pavlenko, 2003) or in perpetuating traditional views of SLA. I have chosen to introduce issues of language, power, identity, and critical approaches to language teaching and learning in this course. The course has as its objectives to help pre-service teachers understand the relationships among intelligibility, accent, and race; challenge the notion of the native speaker and introduce the idea of multicompetence (Cook, 1999), code-switching and code-mixing; introduce issues of language use in relation to gender, class, race, ethnicity, power, and identity; and help understand the connotations of terms like World Englishes,

Table 1. Selected Readings Used over the Years in TESL 570 Educational Sociolinguistics

Global English, World Englishes, English as a Lingua Franca

Burns, A. (2005). Interrogating new worlds of English language teaching. In A. Burns (Ed.), *Teaching English from a global perspective* (pp. 1–15). Alexandria, VA: Teachers of English to Speakers of Other Languages.

Celce-Murcia, M. (2014). Teaching English in the context of world Englishes. In M. Celce-Murcia, D. M. Brinton, & M. A. Snow (Eds.), *Teaching English as a second or a foreign language* (pp. 63–70). Boston: Heinle Cengage Learning.

Friedrich, P., & Matsuda, A. (2010). When five words are not enough: A conceptual and terminological discussion of English as a lingua franca. *International Multilingual Research Journal, 4,* 20–30.

Jenkins, J. (2006), Current perspectives on teaching world Englishes and English as a lingua franca. *TESOL Quarterly, 40*(1), 157–181.

Matsuda, A., & Friedrich, P. (2012). Selecting an instructional variety for an EIL curriculum. In A. Matsuda (Ed.), *Principles and practices of teaching English as an international language* (pp. 17–27). Bristol, U.K.: Multilingual Matters.

McKay, S. L. (2002). *Teaching English as an international language: Rethinking goals and approaches.* Oxford, U.K.: Oxford University Press.

Issues of Identity

Amin, N. (2004). Nativism, the native speaker construct, and minority immigrant women teachers of English as a second language. In L. D. Kamhi-Stein (Ed.), *Learning and teaching from experience: Perspectives on nonnative English-speaking professionals* (pp. 61–80). Ann Arbor: University of Michigan Press.

Golombek, P., & Jordan, S. R. (2005). Becoming "black lambs" not "parrots": A poststructuralist orientation to intelligibility and identity. *TESOL Quarterly, 39*(3), 513–533.

Hansen, J. G. (2004). Invisible minorities and the nonnative English-speaking professional. In L. D. Kamhi-Stein (Ed.), *Learning and teaching from experience: Perspectives on nonnative English-speaking professionals* (pp. 40–55). Ann Arbor: University of Michigan Press.

Kamhi-Stein, L. D. (2014). Non-native English-speaking teachers in the profession. In M. Celce-Murcia, D. M. Brinton, & M. A. Snow (Eds.), *Teaching English as a second or a foreign language* (pp. 586–600). Boston: Heinle Cengage Learning.

Liu, J. (2004). Confessions of a nonnative English-speaking professional. In L. D. Kamhi-Stein (Ed.), *Learning and teaching from experience: Perspectives on nonnative English-speaking professionals* (pp. 25–39). Ann Arbor: University of Michigan Press.

Norton, B. (1997). Language, identity, and the ownership of English. *TESOL Quarterly, 31*(3), 409–429.

Norton, B. (2000). *Identity and language learning: Gender, ethnicity, and educational change.* London: Longman.

Norton, B., & Toohey, K. (2001). Changing perspectives on good language learners. *TESOL Quarterly, 35*(2), 307–322.

Pasternak, M., & Bailey, K. M. (2004). Preparing nonnative and native English-speaking teachers: Issues of professionalism and proficiency. In L. D. Kamhi-Stein (Ed.), *Learning and teaching from experience: Perspective on nonnative English-speaking professionals* (pp. 40–55). Ann Arbor: University of Michigan Press.

Peirce, B. N. (1995). Social identity, investment, and language learning. *TESOL Quarterly, 29*(1), 9–31.

Table 1. Selected Readings Used over the Years in TESL 570 Educational Sociolinguistics (*continued*)

Code-Switching in the Language Classroom

Levine, G. S. (2011). *Code choice in the language classroom.* Bristol, U.K.: Multilingual Matters.

Liu, D., Ahn, G., Baek, K., & Han, N. (2004). South Korean high school English teachers' code switching: Questions and challenges in the drive for maximal use of English in teaching. *TESOL Quarterly, 38*(4), 605–638.

Gender, Language Use, Race, and Ethnicity

Amin, N. (1997). Race and the identity of the nonnative ESL teacher. *TESOL Quarterly, 31*(3), 580–583.

Amin, N. (1999). Minority women teachers of ESL: Negotiating White English. In G. Braine (Ed.), *Non-native educators in English Language Teaching* (pp. 93–104). Mahwah, NJ: Lawrence Erlbaum

Kubota, R., & Lin, A. (2006). Race and TESOL: Introduction to concepts and theories. *TESOL Quarterly, 40*(3), 471–493.

Kubota, R., & Lin, A. (2009). Race, culture, and identities in second language education: Introduction to research and practice. In R. Kubota & A. Lin (Eds.), *Race, culture, and identities in second language education. Exploring critically engaged practice* (pp. 1–23). New York: Routledge.

Losey, K. M. (1995). Gender and ethnicity as factors in the development of verbal skills in bilingual Mexican American women. *TESOL Quarterly, 29*(4), 635–661.

Morita, N. (2004). Negotiating participation and identity in second language academic communities. *TESOL Quarterly, 38,* 573–604.

Motha, S. (2006). Racializing ESOL teacher identities in U.S. K-12 public schools. *TESOL Quarterly, 40*(3), 495–518.

Norton, B., & Pavlenko, A. (2004). Addressing gender in the ESL/EFL classroom. *TESOL Quarterly, 38*(3), 504–514.

English as an international language, English as a lingua franca, and standard varieties of a language.

Over the years I have used several textbooks: *Sociolinguistics and Language Teaching* (McKay & Hornberger, 1996), *Introducing Sociolinguistics* (Meyerhoff, 2006), and *Sociolinguistics and Language Education* (Hornberger & McKay, 2010). The latter is the current text and seems to work well because it emphasizes the relationship between language and power and challenges traditional views of language learning. In addition to the required textbook, students are assigned a variety of articles that supplement the ideas presented in the course textbook. Table 1 presents a list of some of the readings I have used over the years. Not all readings have been used at once. In fact, I have selected

Figure 1. Assessment Criteria for the Autobiographical Narrative

<table>
<tr><th>Assessment Criteria</th><th colspan="2">Points Earned (+ comments)</th></tr>
<tr><td>Content-based criteria</td><td></td><td></td></tr>
<tr><td>The paper may address one or more of the topics, though you are not limited to them. Be selective in the number of topics selected since your paper should be 5-6 pages long. The paper may address factors such as:

language learning experiences in relation to your gender, race, class; your perceptions and/or others' perceptions about your intelligibility, accent, home dialect, or language status; your social standing as well as your educational experiences; factors like the role of English in your community; and issues of culture shock, cultural adaptation, marginalization, empowerment; etc. (as relevant).

The paper must:
• present examples/lessons that illustrate your ideas
• relate your experiences to the sources/readings presented in class (and/or other classes)
• demonstrate a solid understanding of the articles cited
• present reflections/discuss instructional implications and/or beliefs
• make connections between your experiences and beliefs about classroom teaching and learning (as relevant)
• show what you have learned as a professional and/or as a writer from writing the autobiographical narrative</td><td></td><td></td></tr>
<tr><td>Assignment & language-based criteria</td><td></td><td></td></tr>
<tr><td>The paper:
• is written with a TESOL audience in mind (a naïve but educated audience)
• is written from a first-person perspective
• displays references according to APA style guidelines (6th edition)
• includes source materials that are (a) cited appropriately and (b) integrated within the text
• is proofread (for punctuation, spelling, etc.)
• has subheadings to make the text reader-friendly</td><td></td><td></td></tr>
<tr><td></td><td></td><td>TOTAL POINTS:</td></tr>
</table>

different readings from the list over the years, but the ones consistently covered in my classes are those by Peirce (1995), also known as Norton (1997, 2000).

◆ Writing the Narrative: Challenges and Opportunities

The autobiographical narrative is completed at the point when the class has completed a unit on identity. To help pre-service teachers prepare, they also read and discuss the narratives presented in this book, as well as an oral narrative that I presented at a TESOL conference (Kubota, Bashir-Al, Canagarajah, Kamhi-Stein, Lee, & Shin, 2005).

One of the challenges I have had when we get to this point in the course is that the pre-service teachers question the narrative as a source of valid research. I believe that these doubts are a result of the long standing tradition of valuing quantitative research in education and in the research article being the accepted genre of academia. It is not uncommon for my students to take my Educational Sociolinguistics course during their first year in the MA TESOL program, where their other classes have focused on the analysis of research articles that emphasize quantitative data. Research articles have their place in the program to be sure. In fact, in the first few weeks of this course, students are introduced to Swales' (1990) notion of genre analysis and the research article in preparation for a multi-step data collection project (which is the main assignment in the course). The class members read and deconstruct two sample research articles (one quantitative and one qualitative) written by past students. They analyze the introductions of research articles and learn about Swales' (1990) "moves" and his Creating a Research Space (CARS) model (Swales, 1990). They also deconstruct the other sections of the research articles (Literature Review, Method, Results or Findings, and Discussion and Conclusion) and develop an understanding of, for example, the purposes for which the authors use active or passive voice, use various verb tenses, move from general to specific ideas (in the introduction, for example) or vice versa. They analyze rhetorical devices used to signal that the authors are borrowing ideas from prior research (see Barks and Watts, 2001, for examples of class activities). With such a heavy emphasis on the parts of a research article, the fact my students initially question the validity of the autobiographical narrative should, therefore, not come as a surprise.

Another challenge this assignment presents is related. Because they know that research articles rely on survey research and are typically written in the third person, they are reluctant to use the first person and write about themselves and their experiences.

To address these two concerns, the class engages in a series of lively discussions about the notion of objectivity in research. After these discussions, most pre-service teachers (although not all) feel more comfortable with the genre and the assignment.[1]

One surprising opportunity that tends to result from the assignment is that the pre-service teachers are not merely spectators when we discuss research in class; they begin to develop an understanding of the connections between their own lives and the research to which they have been exposed. With greater exposure to the narrative genre, their eyes are opened to the value of research that is not quantitative.

As previously explained, the autobiographical narrative is a powerful tool that can be used to promote teacher reflection and awareness. If students act on the awareness developed, then they can enhance their own instructional practices and their own sense of professionalism as teachers. Clearly, the many opportunities afforded by the autobiographical narrative far outweigh any challenges. Without a doubt, it has resulted in an extremely valuable and powerful assignment for the pre-service teachers.

As a final note, while my pre-service teachers write their autobiographical narratives in my TESL 570 class, the narratives, much like their lives, are not fixed, and continue to evolve. To address this fact, pre-service teachers revisit their narratives in other classes in the program (e.g., Methods of Teaching and Learning Second Languages and

---

[1]Those pre-service teachers who do not feel comfortable writing their narratives in the first person are allowed to do so in the third person without losing points.

Field Work in ESL) and build on them as they write their Teaching Philosophy and their Action Plans as TESOL professionals.

◆ Final Thoughts

As I end this book, I can't help thinking about Angel, Jessie, Hee-Jin, Jeremy, Valerie, and Shannon. I also think about Patty and Quy, the two teachers whose narratives I quoted from in the book (pages 3 and 8). I am reminded of the struggles they all have faced and the successes they have enjoyed. I am reminded that the autobiographical narrative was the tool that first allowed them to reflect on the myriad of connections between their personal lives and their professional lives.

Now it is time for you to embark on the process of reflecting on how your personal experiences inform your instructional practices. My job is done: The book is in your hands. Now, it is time for you to answer a revised version of the question that prompted this book: How can *you* use your own experiences to help your language learners succeed?

Reflection Question

Some pre-service teachers may not feel comfortable discussing issues of race, class, ethnicity, in relation to language teaching. How would you integrate these topics into your course? And how could help these teachers understand the value of reflecting on them when they engage in the writing of their autobiographical narratives?

References

American-Israeli Cooperative Enterprise. (2012). *Virtual Jewish history tour: Argentina.* http://www.jewishvirtuallibrary.org/jsource/vjw/Argentina.html

Amin, N. (1997). Race and the identity of the nonnative ESL teacher. *TESOL Quarterly, 31*(3), 580–583.

Amin, N. (2004). Nativism, the native speaker construct, and minority immigrant women teachers of English as a second language. In L. D. Kamhi-Stein (Ed.), *Learning and teaching from experience: Perspectives on nonnative English-speaking professionals* (pp. 61–80). Ann Arbor: University of Michigan Press.

Auerbach, E. R. (1993). Reexamining English only in the ESL classroom. *TESOL Quarterly, 27,* 9–32.

Barkhuizen, G. (2011). Narrative knowledging in TESOL. *TESOL Quarterly, 45*(3), 391–414.

Barks, D., & Watts, P. (2001). Textual borrowing strategies for graduate-level ESL writers. In D. Belcher & A. Hirvela (Eds.), *Linking literacies: Perspectives on L2 reading-writing connections* (pp. 246–267). Ann Arbor: University of Michigan Press.

Belcher, D., & Connor, U. (Eds.). (2001). *Reflections on multiliterate lives.* Clevedon, U.K.: Multilingual Matters.

Bennett, C. (2001). Genres of research in multicultural education. *Review of Educational Research, 71,* 171–217.

Bhabha, H. K. (1998). Locations of culture. In D.H. Richter (Ed.), *The critical tradition* (2nd ed., pp. 1331–1344). Boston: Bedford.

Bondy, E., & Ross, D. (2008). The teacher as a warm demander. *Educational Leadership, 66*(1), 54–58.

Bourdieu, P. (1994). *Language and symbolic power* (G. Raymond & M. Adamson, Trans.). Cambridge, MA: Harvard University Press. (Original work published 1977).

Braine, G. (2010). *Nonnative speaker English teachers: Research, pedagogy, and professional growth.* New York: Routledge.

Braine, G. (1999). *Non-native educators in English language teaching.* Mahwah, NJ: Lawrence Erlbaum.

Braine, G., Canagarajah, S., Connor, U., Sridhar, K., Thomas, J., & Chipatru, D. (1996, March). *In their own voices: Nonnative speaker professionals in TESOL.* Colloquium presented at the annual meeting of the Teachers of English to Speakers of Other Languages, Chicago: IL.

Braine, G., Liu, J., & Kamhi-Stein, L. D. (1998). *Statement of purpose: Nonnative English-speaking teachers caucus.* Retrieved from http://www.tesol.org/connect/interest-sections/nonnative-english-speakers-in-tesol

Briggs, C. (1998). "You're a liar—You're just like a woman!" In B. B. Schieffelin, K. A. Woolard, & P. V. Kroskrity (Eds.), *Language ideologies: Practice and theory* (pp. 229–255). New York: Oxford University Press.

Brown, G. (1990). Cultural values: The interpretation of discourse. *ELT Journal, 44*(1), 11–24.

Burns, A. (2005). Interrogating new worlds of English language teaching. In A. Burns (Ed.), *Teaching English from a global perspective* (pp. 1–15). Alexandria, VA: Teachers of English to Speakers of Other Languages.

Butler, Y. G. (2007). How are non-native English speaking teachers perceived by young learners? *TESOL Quarterly 41*(4), 731–755.

Canagarajah, A. S. (1996). From critical research practice to critical research reporting. *TESOL Quarterly, 30*(2), 321–331.

Canagarajah, A. S. (1999). *Resisting linguistic imperialism in English teaching.* New York: Oxford University Press.

Canagarajah, A. S. (2005). Introduction. In A. S. Canagarajah (Ed.), *Reclaiming the local in language policy and practice* (pp. xiii–xxx). Mahwah, NJ: Lawrence Erlbaum.

Casanave, C. P., & Schecter, S. R. (Eds.). (1997). *On becoming a language educator: Personal essays on professional development.* Mahwah, NJ: Lawrence Erlbaum.

Chacón, C. (2009). Transforming the curriculum of NNESTs: Introducing critical language awareness (CLA) in a teacher education program. In R. Kubota & A. Lin, (Eds.), *Race, culture, and identities in second language education. Exploring critically engaged practice* (pp. 215–233). New York: Routledge.

Chang, S. (2004). *A case study of EFL teachers in Taiwan: Identities, instructional practice and intercultural awareness.* Retrieved from ProQuest Digital Dissertations. (AAT 3129849)

Choi, S. J. (2007). *The experiences of non-native English speaking teachers and their professional identity constructions in an ESL context.* Retrieved from ProQuest Digital Dissertations. (AAT 3301115)

Chubbuck, S. (2004). Whiteness enacted, whiteness disrupted: The complexity of personal congruence. *American Educational Research Journal, 41,* 301–333.

Cisneros, S. (1991). *The house on mango street* (2nd ed.). Millers Falls, MA: Vintage.

Clandinin, D. J., & Connelly, F. M. (Eds.). (1995). *Teachers' professional knowledge landscapes.* New York: Teachers College Press.

Clandinin, D. J., & Connelly, F. M. (2000). *Narrative inquiry: Experience and story in qualitative research.* San Francisco: Jossey-Bass.

Clandinin, D. J., Pushor, D., & Orr, A. M. (2007). Navigating sites for narrative inquiry. *Journal of Teacher Education, 58*(1), 21–35.

Clark, E., & Paran, A. (2007). The employability of non-native-speaker teachers of EFL: A UK survey. *System, 35*(4), 407-430.

Clark, E. R., & Flores, B. B. (2001). Who am I? The social construction of ethnic identity and self-perceptions of bilingual preservice teachers. *The Urban Review, 33*(2), 69–86.

Cohen, R. (1997). *Global diasporas.* Seattle: University of Washington Press.

Connelly, F. M., & Clandinin, D. J. (1990). Stories of experience and narrative inquiry. *Educational Researcher, 19*(5), 2–14.

Connelly, F. M., & Clandinin, D. J. (Eds.) (1999). *Shaping a professional identity: Stories of educational practice.* New York: Teachers College Press.

Cook, V. (1999). Going beyond the native speaker in language teaching. *TESOL Quarterly, 33,* 185–209.

Cook, V. (2001). Using first language in the classroom. *Canadian Modern Language Review, 57,* 402–423.

Cook, V. (n.d.). *Evidence for multi-competence.* Retrieved from http://homepage.ntlworld.com/vivian.c/SLA/Multicompetence/MCEvidence.htm

Curtis, M., & Romney, M. (Eds.). (2006). *Color, race, and English language teaching: Shades of meaning.* Mahwah, NJ: Lawrence Erlbaum.

Delpit, L. (2006a). *Other people's children: Cultural conflict in the classroom* (2nd ed.). New York: The New Press.

Delpit, L. (2006b). What should teachers do? Ebonics and culturally responsive instruction. In S. Nero (Ed.), *Dialects, Englishes, creoles, and education* (pp. 93–101). New York: Lawrence Erlbaum.

Dome, N., Prado-Olmos, P., Ulanoff, S., Garcia Ramos, R., Vega-Castaneda, L. & Quiocho, A. (2005). I don't like not knowing how the world works: Examining preservice teachers' narrative reflections. *Teacher Education Quarterly, 32,* 63–83.

Duff, P. A. (2001). Language, literacy, content, and (pop) culture: Challenges for ESL students in mainstream courses. *The Canadian Modern Language Review, 59,* 103–132.

Duff, P. A. (2002). The discursive co-construction of knowledge, identity, and difference: An ethnography of communication in high school mainstream. *Applied Linguistics, 23,* 289–322.

Duff, P. A., & Uchida, Y. (1997). The negotiation of teachers' sociocultural identities and practices in postsecondary EFL classrooms. *TESOL Quarterly, 31*(3), 451–486.

Eckert, P., & McConnel-Ginet, S. (1992). Think practically and look locally: Language and gender as a community-based practice. *Annual Review of Anthropology, 21,* 461–490.

Elbaz-Luwisch, F. (2007). Studying teacher's lives and experience: Narrative inquiry into K-12 teaching. In D. J. Clandinin (Ed.), *Handbook of narrative inquiry: Mapping a methodology* (pp. 357–382). Thousand Oaks, CA: Sage.

Ellis, R. (1994). *The study of second language acquisition.* Oxford: Oxford University Press.

Ferguson, C. A. (1959). Diglossia. *Word, 15,* 325–340.

Fishman, J. A. (1972). *The sociology of language.* Rowley, MA: Newbury House.

Foucault, M. (1984). *Of other spaces: Heterotopia* (J. Miskowiec, Trans.). Retrieved from http://foucault.info/documents/heteroTopia/foucault.heteroTopia.en.html (Original work published 1967).

Freire, P. (1990). *Pedagogy of the oppressed* (M. B. Ramos, Trans.). (Original work published 1972). New York: Continuum.

Flynn, J. E. (2010). Discussing race and culture in the middle-school classroom. In S. May & C. E. Sleeter (Eds.), *Critical multiculturalism: Theory and praxis* (pp. 165–175). New York: Routledge.

Garrett, T., Barr, J., & Rothman, T. (2009). Perspectives on caring in the classroom: Do they vary according to ethnicity or grade level? *Adolescence, 44*(175), 505–521.

Gay, G. (2000). *Culturally responsive teaching: Theory, research, and practice.* New York: Teachers College Press.

Gay, G. (2002). Preparing for culturally responsive teaching. *Journal of Teacher Education,* 106–116.

Gay, G. (2010). *Culturally responsive teaching (2nd. ed.).* New York: Teachers College Press.

Gollnick, D., & Chinn, P. (2002). *Multicultural education in a pluralistic society* (6th ed.). Upper Saddle River, NJ: Merrill Prentice Hall.

Golombek, P., & Jordan, S. R. (2005). Becoming "black lambs" not "parrots": A poststructuralist orientation to intelligibility and identity. *TESOL Quarterly, 39*(3), 513–533.

Hachey, A. C. (2012). Care from a cognitive perspective. *Knowledge Quest, 40*(4), 38–44.

Hansen, J. G. (2004). Invisible minorities and the nonnative English-speaking professional. In L. D. Kamhi-Stein (Ed.), *Learning and teaching from experience: Perspectives on nonnative English–speaking professionals* (pp. 40–55). Ann Arbor: University of Michigan Press.

Holmes, J. (2001). *An introduction to sociolinguistics* (2nd ed.). Harlow, U.K.: Longman.

Hornberger, N. H., & McKay, S. L. (Eds.). (2010). *Sociolinguistics and language education*. Bristol, U.K.: Multilingual Matters.

Hughes, L. (Ed.). (1967). *The best short stories by black writers, 1899–1967: The classic anthology.* Boston: Little, Brown and Company.

Ilieva, R. (2010). Non-native English-speaking teachers' negotiations of program discourses in their construction of professional identities within a TESOL program. *The Canadian Modern Language Review/La Revue Canadienne des langues vivantes, 66*(3), 343–369.

Jenkins, J. (2005). Implementing an international approach to English pronunciation: The role of teacher attitudes and identity. *TESOL Quarterly, 39*(3), 535–543.

Jenkins, J. (2006). Current perspectives on teaching world Englishes and English as a lingua franca. *TESOL Quarterly, 40*(1), 157–181.

Johnson, L. (2002). "My eyes have been opened": White teachers and racial awareness. *Journal of Teacher Education, 53,* 153–167.

Johnson, K. E. (2006). The sociocultural turn and its challenges for second language teacher education. *TESOL Quarterly, 40*(1), 235–257.

Johnson, K. E., & Golombek, P. R. (2002). *Teachers' narrative inquiry as professional development.* New York: Cambridge University Press.

Johnson, K. E., & Golombek, P. R. (2011). The transformative power of narrative in second language teacher education. *TESOL Quarterly, 45*(3), 486–509.

Jung, S. K., & Norton, B. (2002). Language planning in Korea: The new elementary English program. In J. W. Tollefson (Ed.), *Language policies in education* (pp. 245–265). Mahwah, NJ: Lawrence Erlbaum.

Kachru, B. B. (1992). Teaching World Englishes. In B. B. Kachru (Ed.), *The other tongue: English across cultures* (2nd ed.) (pp. 355–365), Chicago: University of Illinois Press.

Kachru, B. B. (1996). The paradigms of marginality. *World Englishes, 15*(3), 241–255.

Kachru, B., & Nelson, C. (1996). World Englishes. In S. L. McKay & N. H. Hornberger (Eds.), *Sociolinguistics and language teaching* (pp. 71–102). Cambridge, U.K.: Cambridge University Press.

Kachru, Y., & Smith, L. E. (2008), *Cultures, contexts, and World Englishes*. New York: Routledge.

Kamhi-Stein, L. D. (1999). Preparing nonnative English-speaking professionals in TESOL: Implications for teacher education programs. In G. Braine (Ed.), *Non-native educators in ELT* (pp. 147–160). Mahwah, NJ: Lawrence Erlbaum.

Kamhi-Stein, L. D. (2000). Looking to the future of TESOL teacher education: Integrating Web-based bulletin board discussions into the methods course. *TESOL Quarterly, 34*(3), 423-456.

Kamhi-Stein, L. D. (2014). Non-native English-speaking teachers in the profession. In M. Celce-Murcia, D. M. Brinton, & M. A. Snow (Eds.), *Teaching English as a second or foreign language* (pp. 586–600). Boston: Heinle Cengage Learning.

Kamwangamalu, N. M. (2010). Multilingualism and codeswitching in education. In N. H. Hornberger & S. L. McKay (Eds.), *Sociolinguistics and language education* (pp. 116–142). Bristol, U.K.: Multilingual Matters.

Kanno, Y., & Norton, B. (2003). Imagined communities and educational possibilities: Introduction. *Journal of Language, Identity, and Education, 2*(4), 241–249.

Kasper, G., & Omori, M. (2010). Language and culture. In N. H. Hornberger & S. L. McKay (Eds.), *Sociolinguistics and language education* (pp. 455–491). Bristol, U.K.: Multilingual Matters.

Kemp, H. R., & Reupert, A. (2012). "There is not big book on how to care": Primary pre-service teachers' experiences of caring. *Australian Journal of Teacher Education, 37*(9), 114–127.

Kim, L. S. (2003). Multiple identities in a multicultural world: A Malaysian perspective. *Journal of Language, Identity, and Education, 2*(3), 137–158.

Kim, T. (2008). Accentedness, comprehensibility, intelligibility, and interpretability of NNESTs. *The CATESOL Journal, 20*(1), 7–26.

Kristeva, J. (1991). *Strangers to ourselves* (L. S. Roudiez, Trans.). New York: Columbia University Press.

Kubota, R., Bashir-Al, K.I., Canagarajah, S., Kamhi-Stein, L. D., Lee, E., & Shin, H. (2005). Race and (non)nativeness in English language teaching: A brief report. *NNEST Newsletter, 7*(2). Retrieved from http://www.tesol.org/read-and-publish/newsletters-other-publications/interest-section-newsletters/nnest-newsletter/2011/10/27/nnest-news-volume-7-2-(October-2005)

Kubota, R., & Lin, A. (2006). Race and TESOL: Introduction to concepts and theories. *TESOL Quarterly, 40*(3), 471–493.

Kubota, R., & Lin, A. (2009). Race, culture, and identities in second language education: Introduction to research and practice. In R. Kubota & A. Lin, (Eds.), *Race, culture, and identities in second language education. Exploring critically engaged practice* (pp. 1–23). New York: Routledge.

Kumaravadivelu, B. (2001). Toward a postmethod pedagogy. *TESOL Quarterly, 35*(4), 537–560.

Lea, V. (2010). Empowering pre-service teachers, students, and families through critical multiculturalism: Interweaving social foundations of education and community action projects. In S. May & C. E. Sleeter (Eds.), *Critical multiculturalism: Theory and praxis* (pp. 33–45). New York: Routledge.

Levine, G. S. (2011). *Code choice in the language classroom*. Bristol, U.K.: Multilingual Matters.

Liu, D., Ahn, G., Baek, K., & Han, N. (2004). South Korean high school English teachers' code switching: Questions and challenges in the drive for maximal use of English in teaching. *TESOL Quarterly, 38*(4), 605–638.

Liu, J. (1999). Nonnative-English speaking professionals. *TESOL Quarterly, 33*, 85–102.

Liu, J. (2004). Confessions of a nonnative English–speaking professional. In L. D. Kamhi-Stein (Ed.), *Learning and teaching from experience: Perspectives on nonnative English–speaking professionals* (pp. 25–39). Ann Arbor: University of Michigan Press.

Losey, K. M. (1995). Gender and ethnicity as factors in the development of verbal skills in bilingual Mexican American women. *TESOL Quarterly, 29*(4), 635–661.

Losey, K. M. (1997). *Listen to the silences: Mexican American interaction in the composition classroom and community*. Norwood, NJ: Ablex.

Lu, Y. (2005). *Stories of teacher identity: A narrative inquiry into East Asian ESL teachers' lives.* Retrieved from ProQuest Digital Dissertations. (AAT 3201975)

MacNeil, R., & Cran, W. (2005). *Do you speak American?* New York: Nan A. Talese.

Mahboob, A. (2004). Native or nonnative: What do students enrolled in an intensive English program think? In L. D. Kamhi-Stein (Ed.), *Learning and teaching from experience: Perspectives on nonnative English–speaking professionals* (pp. 40–55). Ann Arbor: University of Michigan Press.

Matsuda, A. (2003a). The ownership of English in Japanese secondary schools. *World Englishes, 22*(4), 483–496.

Matsuda, A. (2003b). Incorporating world Englishes in teaching English as an international language. *TESOL Quarterly, 37*(4), 719–727.

Matsuda, A. (Ed.) (2012). *Principles and practices of teaching English as an international language.* Bristol, U.K.: Multilingual Matters.

May, S. (2005). Language rights: Moving the debate forward. *Journal of Sociolinguistics, 9*(3), 319–347.

Mazzei, L. (1997, March). *Making our white selves intelligible to ourselves: Implications for teacher education.* Paper presented at the Annual Meeting of the American Educational Research Association, Chicago, IL.

McKay, S. L. (2002). *Teaching English as an international language: Rethinking goals and approaches.* Oxford, U.K.: Oxford University Press.

McKay, S. L., & Hornberger, N. H. (Eds.). (1996). *Sociolinguistics and language teaching.* Cambridge, U.K.: Cambridge University Press.

Medgyes, P. (1992). Native or non-native: Who's worth more? *ELT Journal, 46*(1), 340–349.

Medgyes, P. (2001). When the teacher is a nonnative speaker. In M. Celce-Murcia (Ed.), *Teaching English as a second or foreign language* (pp. 429–442). Boston: Heinle and Heinle.

Mehan, H. (1982). The structure of classroom events and their consequences for student performance. In P. Gilmore & D. M. Smith (Eds.), *Children in and out of school: Ethnography and education* (pp. 59–87). Cambridge, MA: Harvard University Press.

Menard-Warwick, J. (2011). A methodological reflection on the process of narrative analysis: Alienation and identity in the life histories of English language teachers. *TESOL Quarterly, 45*(3), 564–574.

Meyerhoff, M. (2006). *Introducing sociolinguistics.* New York: Routledge.

Morita, N. (2004). Negotiating participation and identity in second language academic communities. *TESOL Quarterly, 38,* 573–603.

Motha, S. (2006). Racializing ESOL teacher identities in U.S. K-12 public schools. *TESOL Quarterly, 40*(3), 495–518.

Newmeyer, F. J. (1973). Linguistic theory, language teaching, sociolinguistics: Can they be interrelated? *The Modern Language Journal, 57*(8), 405–410.

Noblit, G. W. (1993). Power and caring. *American Educational Research Journal, 30*(1), 23–38.

Norton, B. (1997). Language, identity, and the ownership of English. *TESOL Quarterly, 31*(3), 409–429.

Norton, B. (2000). *Identity and language learning: Gender, ethnicity, and educational change.* London: Longman.

Norton, B., & Toohey, K. (2001). Changing perspectives on good language learners. *TESOL Quarterly, 35*(2), 307–322.

Nunan, D., & Choi, J. (Eds.). (2010). *Language and culture: Reflective narratives and the emergence of identity.* New York: Routledge.

Pasternak, M., & Bailey, K. M. (2004). Preparing nonnative and native English-speaking teachers: Issues of professionalism and proficiency. In L. D. Kamhi-Stein (Ed.), *Learning and teaching from experience: Perspectives on nonnative English–speaking professionals* (pp. 40–55). Ann Arbor: University of Michigan Press.

Pavlenko, A. (2003). "I never knew I was a bilingual": Reimagining teacher identities in TESOL. *Journal of Language, Identity, and Education, 2*(2), 251–268.

Peirce, B. N. (1995). Social identity, investment, and language learning. *TESOL Quarterly, 29*(1), 9–31.

Pennycook, A. (2001). *Critical applied linguistics: A critical introduction.* Mahwah, NJ: Lawrence Erlbaum.

Pennycook, A. (2007). *Global Englishes and transcultural flows.* New York: Routledge.

Phillipson, R. (1994). *Linguistic imperialism.* Oxford, U.K.: Oxford University Press.

Prodromou, L. (1992). What culture? Which culture? Cross-cultural factors in language learning. *ELT Journal, 46,* 39–50.

Raible, J., & Irizarry, J. (2007). Transracialized selves and the emergence of post-white teacher identities. *Race, Ethnicity, and Education, 10,* 177–198.

Reyes, A. (2010). Language and ethnicity. In N. H. Hornberger & S. L. McKay (Eds.), *Sociolinguistics and language education.* Bristol, U.K.: Multilingual Matters.

Rubin, J. (1975). What the "good language learner" can teach us. *TESOL Quarterly, 9,* 41–51.

Saito, T. (2005). *Exploring nonnative-English-speaking teachers' experiences in teaching English at a United States university.* Retrieved from ProQuest Digital Dissertations. (AAT 3205468)

Samimy, K. K., & Brutt-Griffler, J. (1999). To be a native or non-native speaker: Perceptions of "non-native" students in a graduate TESOL program. In G. Braine (Ed.), *Non-native educators in English language teaching* (pp. 127–144). Mahwah, NJ: Lawrence Erlbaum.

Schumann, J. (1978). The acculturation model for second language acquisition. In R. Gingras (Ed.), *Second language acquisition and foreign language teaching* (pp. 27–50). Arlington, VA: Center for Applied Linguistics.

Scott, V. M., & de la Fuente, M. J. (2008). What's the problem? L2 learners' use of the L1 during consciousness-raising. *The Modern Language Journal, 92*(1), 100–113.

Selvi, A. F. (2010). All teachers are equal, but some teachers are more equal than others: Trend analysis of job advertisements in English language teaching. *WATESOL NNEST Caucus Annual Review, 1,* 156–181.

Sleeter, C. (2005). How white teachers construct race. In C. McCarthy, W. Crichlow, G. Dimitriadis, & N. Dolby (Eds.), *Race, identity, and representation in education* (2nd ed., pp. 243–257). New York: Routledge.

Sleeter, C. E. & Owuor, J. (2011). Research on the impact of teacher preparation to teach diverse students: The research we have and the research we need. *Action in Teacher Education, 33,* 524–536.

Spada, N., & Fröhlich, M. (1995). *The communicative orientation of language teaching observation scheme.* Sydney, Australia: Macquarie University, National Centre for English Language Teaching and Research.

Sridhar, K. (1996). Societal multilingualism. In S. L. McKay & N. H. Hornberger (Eds.), *Sociolinguistics and language teaching* (pp. 47–70). Cambridge, U.K.: Cambridge University Press.

Swales, J. M. (1990). *Genre analysis: English in academic and research settings.* Cambridge, U.K.: Cambridge University Press.

Tan, G. (2001). I want my teachers to like me: Multiculturalism and school dropout rates among Mexican Americans. *Equity & Excellence in Education, 34,* 35–42.

Trumbull, E., & Pacheco, M. (2005). *Leading with diversity: Cultural competencies for teacher preparation and professional development.* Boston: Brown University and Pacific Resources for Education.

Tsui, A. B. M. (2007). The complexities of identity formation: A narrative inquiry of an EFL teacher. *TESOL Quarterly, 41*(4), 657–680.

U.S. Department of Education. (2011). *Our future, our teachers: The Obama administration's plan for teacher education reform and improvement.* Retrieved from www.ed.gov/sites/default/files/our-future-our-teachers.pdf

Valdes, J. M. (1986). *Culture bound.* Cambridge, U.K.: Cambridge University Press.

Vandrick, S. (2009). *Integrating privilege: Reflections of a second language educator.* Ann Arbor: University of Michigan Press.

Varghese, M., Morgan, B., Johnston, B., & Johnson, K. A. (2005). Theorizing language teacher identity: Three perspectives and beyond. *Journal of Language, Identity, and Education, 4,* 21–44.

Vavrus, M. (2002, November). *Connecting teacher identity formation to culturally responsive teaching.* Paper presented at the Annual Meeting of the National Association of Multicultural Education, Washington, DC.

Vázquez, C. (2011). TESOL, teacher identity, and the need for "small" story research. *TESOL Quarterly, 45*(3), 535–545.

Velasco-Martin, C. (2004). The nonnative English-speaking teacher as an intercultural speaker. In L. D. Kamhi-Stein (Ed.), *Learning and teaching from experience: Perspectives on nonnative English–speaking professionals* (pp. 277–293). Ann Arbor: University of Michigan Press.

Weedon, C. (1987). *Feminist practice and poststructionalist theory.* New York: Blackwell.

Wenden, A., & Rubin, J. (Eds.). (1987). *Learner strategies in language learning.* Englewood Cliffs, NY: Prentice-Hall International.

Widdowson, H. (1994). The ownership of English. *TESOL Quarterly, 28*(2), 377–389.

Biographical Statements[1]

Lía D. Kamhi-Stein, Ph.D., California State University, Los Angeles. I am originally from Argentina where I was an EFL learner. I graduated from Universidad del Salvador with a degree as a Certified Public Translator (CPT) but decided to obtain an EFL teaching degree from the same university because I felt isolated and unfulfilled working as a translator. My teaching career started without professional preparation when I was 18 years old and continued while I was studying to become a CPT. After teaching for several different British English-oriented institutes and obtaining my teaching degree, I was hired to teach EFL at Instituto Cultural Argentino Norteamericano (the Buenos Aires, Binational Center), where I later became an academic coordinator and an academic secretary (an academic position). I married my husband, a Business and Law librarian at California State University, Los Angeles, and migrated to Southern California where I have lived since 1990. I am a professor in the TESOL M.A. program at California State University, Los Angeles, and have published articles, chapters, and edited volumes. I am a co-founding member of the TESOL's NNEST Caucus (now an interest section) (with G. Braine and J. Liu) and served as President of CATESOL (2002–2003) and as Member-at-Large on TESOL's Board of Directors (2004–2007). More importantly, I am Hannah's mom.

Valerie J. Callet, Ed.D., Orange County Department of Education. I decided I wanted to be a teacher when I was in 7th grade. I completed my Bachelor's in Education at Penn State University. Then I joined

[1]The authors' affiliations in this section are the ones the authors held in June 2013. The affiliations provided in their narratives are those the authors had at the time they wrote their autobiographical narratives.

the Peace Corps where I taught EFL in Bulgaria and met and married my husband (a Bulgarian). Our daughter Ani was born in 2010. In the United States, I taught English in an alternative education program (the one described in this book) while earning my Master's in TESOL at California State University, Los Angeles. Later, I earned a Doctorate at the University of Southern California. I have taught in a variety of settings, but my passion is teaching at risk youth.

Jessie Chen, CEO, Asian Debate League, Taipei, Taiwan. I am originally from Korea and immigrated to the U.S. when I was 11 years old as a 5th grader. I started out my middle school years as an ESL learner in Los Angeles School District. I graduated from California State University, Los Angeles, with a Bachelor's Degree in English Literature, and with a credential to teach high school English. However, I decided to further pursue my master's in TESOL from the same university because I wanted to be able to teach ESL students. My teaching career started while I was still working on my M.A. thesis. I was hired by Santee High School in the Los Angeles Unified School District and taught high school English for a couple of years; during this time, I successfully organized and coached a high school debate team that won 4th place in 2008 and 2nd place in the 2009 Global Debates competition. In 2010, I moved to Taipei, Taiwan, to rejoin my husband and kids after six years of separation and started my own debate academy. In 2012, two of my Taipei Debate Academy students received the National Junior Forensics League award.

Jeremy C. Kelley, Ph.D. Candidate, Applied Linguistics Program, University of California, at Los Angeles. As a doctoral candidate in applied linguistics at the University of California, Los Angeles, I have taught a range of English as a second or foreign language courses, as well as undergraduate applied linguistics courses for the departmental major. I currently teach as an adjunct professor within the MA TESOL program at California State University, Los Angeles, where I have had the pleasure of training graduate students in preparation for their future careers as language teaching professionals. My primary research interests include first and second language teaching/pedagogy, the ethnography of communication, and discourse analysis as a methodological practice.

Hee-Jin Kim, Teachers College, Columbia University in New York City. I was born and raised in Seoul, Korea, but also spent some time growing up in the U.S. In addition, I lived in Wuerzburg, Germany, for one year when I took some time off from college. After resigning from a big corporate desk job, teaching was only a part time job that would hold me over until I found my next big thing. Little did I know my next big thing would be more teaching and more studying to be better at it. After graduating from California State University, Los Angeles, with my MA in TESOL, I was hired at the American Language and Culture Institute at California State University, San Marcos. I taught ESL for 3 years before deciding to go back to graduate school. Now I am an Ed.M. (Master's of Education) student at Teachers College, Columbia University.

Shannon Ladymon, Sierra School. Since childhood, I have loved languages and made it a point to study as many as possible. Teaching ESL is the perfect extension of that love of languages. I received my B.A. in Linguistics from the University of California, Santa Barbara, followed by my M.A. in TESOL from California State University, Los Angeles. I then taught EFL in Japan for two years before coming back to California, where I now teach exchange students from countries such as China and Korea at a small private school. I also study new languages in my free time.

Veneza Angel Pablico, English Language Program, California State University, Los Angeles, and Glendale Community College. I spent my childhood and early teens in Manila, the Philippines, before immigrating to the United States in 1998. I then graduated from the University of Oklahoma in 2002 with a bachelor's degree in English and a minor in History. After college, I decided to pursue a teaching career, so I attended California State University, Los Angeles, and completed my M.A. in TESOL in 2005. In that same year I started teaching at Cal State–L.A.'s English Language Program (ELP) and Glendale Community College's Credit ESL Division. I have been an ESL Instructor at both institutions since then, and I am currently serving as the Reading & College Success Curriculum Coordinator in the ELP. I am also an active member of CATESOL and have given presentations at its annual conferences. In 2011, I completed a second master's degree in Library & Information Science from San Jose State University, and I plan to work as a part-time college librarian.

Subject Index

Author Index